PERSONAL REMINISCENCES

of

CHARLES HADDON SPURGEON

by

William Williams

Eagle Wing Publications

PERSONAL REMINISCENCES OF CHARLES HADDON SPURGEON
© Copyright Eagle Wing Publications 2014

All rights reserved

ISBN 978 1 909751 15 6

No part of this book may be reproduced, stored in a retrieval system, or transmitted in any form or by any means - electronic, mechanical, photocopy, recording, or otherwise - without written permission of the publisher, except for brief quotation in written reviews.

Printed by
jcprintltd
BELFAST
Telephone 07860 205333
Fax 028 9079 0420
email: info@jcprint.net

PUBLISHERS NOTE

From his youth until his old age Spurgeon had one theme as a preacher of the Everlasting Gospel, Jesus Christ and Him Crucified. He died at 57 years old worn out with labours and cast down with sickness, his advice was "Learn to love the burdens Christ gives you to bear."

In sending forth this reprint of "Personal Reminiscences of Charles Haddon Spurgeon" the present publishers trust it will prove to be of lasting blessing to the reader.

The author William Williams, a personal friend of Spurgeon, preached in Upton Chapel London, a church planted by Spurgeon and it is said that his preaching "attracted a considerable congregation almost under the shadow of the Metropolitan Tabernacle."

All profits from the sale of this book will go to support Mourne Independent Christian School.

I dedicate its reprint to the memory of my mother, Susan, who died in her 90th year, from whom I acquired a love of reading good books.

George McConnell

George McConnell
EAGLE WING PUBLICATIONS

EAGLE WING PUBLICATIONS
4 Church Road
Carrigenagh
Kilkeel
County Down
Northern Ireland BT34 4QB

Email:eaglewingpublications@gmail.com

First published by the Religious Tract Society 1895

PREFACE

'I BELIEVE God sent you to "Upton" for my sake,' Mr. Spurgeon once said to me in the exuberance of his love. I took little notice of the words at the time, but have wondered since whether I was not brought to London that I might, with other service, render, by Divine ordaining, the following tribute to his honoured name. I cannot but think that it was really so. I therefore confidently look for the blessing of God upon this labour of love.

I believe also that a gracious Providence ordered the time when this tribute should be written; for the pleasant task has been accomplished during a season of exceptional bereavements and family sorrow. It has thus engaged the mind with memories of many sunny hours, when otherwise it might have brooded to its own hurt over prevailing griefs. John Bright has told us how Richard Cobden found him sitting alone, with a breaking heart over the loss of his wife, and by urging him to take part in the enterprise of bringing bread to the hungry and the poor, gave a new interest to his life. So often has it been that God has called to extra service as a relief from sorrow. How good a God He is!

The Society did not want too large a book, and so I have been obliged to condense and compress, and also to omit many things which might otherwise have been recorded; but as those given are a fair sample of the whole of the reminiscences preserved, I have little to regret in this.

The effort throughout the work has been to describe Mr. Spurgeon exactly as he was, and to record his sayings exactly as he uttered them. That the picture may be complete, occasional references are made both to living persons and also to subjects not usually referred to in the Society's publications. Some of these references are most characteristic of the man. It is hardly needful to state, but to avoid misunderstanding it may be well to note, that the Society is not to be taken as necessarily endorsing statements which have been allowed to remain because they are so characteristic of the great preacher.

Reader, may the faith, and love, and heart consecration of C. H. Spurgeon be both thine and mine!

W. WILLIAMS

CONTENTS

		Page
I	Introduction	9
II	The Charm Of His Friendship	19
III	Sunny Memories	54
IV	Rural Rambles	75
V	The Peerless President	111
VI	Table Talk	138
VII	His Choice Correspondence	185
VIII	The Famous Preacher	213
IX	Sermon Sapplings	243

LIST OF ILLUSTRATIONS

	Page
Facsimile Of A Letter From Mr Spurgeon	55
The Mole	83
Beddington Village	83
Beddington Church	88
Emancipation Oak	94
Town Court, Oprington	96
Benmore	101
A Group Of Students At The Pastor's College	112
A Lesson To A Student	132
Facsimile Of A Letter From Mr Spurgeon	193
Facsimile Of The Notes From Which The Sermon On Mark 1:45 Was Preached	222
Old Memorial Tablet In Okewood Church	226
Okewood Church Porch	229
One Of The Paths To Okewood Church	229
Rustic Bridge Near Okewood Church	231
Path To Okewood Church	231
Facsimile Of The Notes From Which The Sermon On Matthew 25:32 Was Preached	234

Personal Reminiscences
of
CH SPURGEON

CHAPTER I

INTRODUCTION

LORD MACAULAY, in his essay on John Milton, has so exactly expressed my own sentiments as I contemplate describing my personal reminiscences of C. H. Spurgeon, that I cannot do better than transcribe his words: 'We are not much in the habit of idolising either the living or the dead, and we think there is no more certain indication of a weak and irregulated intellect than that propensity which, for want of a better name, we will venture to christen Boswellism. But there are a few characters which have stood the closest scrutiny and the severest tests, which have been tried in the furnace and have proved pure, which have been weighed in the balance and have not been found wanting, which have been declared sterling by the general consent of mankind, and which are visibly stamped with the image and superscription of the Most High. These great men, we trust, we know how to prize.'

'If you receive the heart of a friend,' I once heard Mr. Spurgeon say, 'mind you give him back your own.' I count it one of the highest privileges of my life that I was one of many received into the big, brotherly heart of this mighty man of God. That I had given him back my own was a fact which came home to me with startling reality when the dear companion of many an hour-sunlit and inspired by the matchless charm of his character had passed within the veil. This earth must henceforth be poorer since he has left it; while heaven is stronger in its attractions since he is there.

> When such friends part,
> 'Tis the survivor dies.

During the first months which succeeded his death I frequently turned to my precious treasury of notes, wherein I had preserved many of the choice utterances, the wise and witty sayings, of my friend. How grateful I felt that I had done so! for his talk had dust of gold, or it resembled 'those celestial fruits and flowers which the virgin martyr of Massinger sent down from the gardens of Paradise to the earth, and which were distinguished from the productions of other soils, not only by superior bloom and sweetness, but by miraculous efficacy to invigorate and to heal. They were powerful not only to delight, but to elevate and purify.'

Very many of Mr. Spurgeon's most characteristic utterances cannot be made public. To do so would be a betrayal of the sacred privileges of friendship. Such sayings must, however, always remain a rich heritage of joy and fun to their possessor. I was giving a specimen one day of his talk, which must be withheld from print, to a minister. He laughed to tears, and said, 'How splendid! What a pity you cannot give these things to the public! But you cannot.' Yet I have others, pearls of speech, which I can give, and which to record will involve no breach of solemn trust. A perusal of them can only tend to the pleasure and the blessing of the reader. And this I hope to do without laying myself open to a charge of 'Boswellism.'

Yet, lest this reservation be misunderstood, I venture to say that if all Mr. Spurgeon's conversations were given to the world, they could but enhance the public estimate both of his goodness and his greatness. Only a few months before the illness which terminated in his death, his reply to a letter containing something in the nature of a threat was 'You may write my life across the sky; I have nothing to conceal.' This is a true portraiture of the good man's life - Nothing to conceal. 'It is a great thing,' says one, 'to have no secret like a lie in the life.' This man most assuredly had no such secret in his life. When the dentist put his first false tooth in he said to me, 'It is the first false thing I have harboured in my mouth.' All his talk was honesty personified; his life was transparent as a sunbeam; his spirit guileless as that of the 'Israelite indeed.' Grace seldom, if ever, produced a character which, for sterling integrity, for unsullied purity and noble generosity, excelled that of C. H. Spurgeon.

Many authors have written of Mr. Spurgeon; and have dealt at length with his ancestry, his infancy and youth, and with his unique career as preacher, author, philanthropist, and pastor. I do not, therefore, propose, in this volume, to retraverse these well-worn paths; although much might be penned, and doubtless one day will be, which each and every biographer has failed to secure and record. But with the main events of his history the world at large has long been made familiar. It is questionable if the career of any public man has been more minutely and fully preserved in the public annals of his time than that of this great Englishman and greater Christian. Ever since he first burst upon the life of England like some strange and brilliant star, to the day of his decease, almost his every movement and public utterance have been noted and recorded. A life, full and fairly accurate, might be written from the almost infinite variety of articles in newspapers, magazines, and pamphlets concerning him. I venture to say that it is a fact unique in the world's history, that any preacher of the Gospel should thus have had his life written for him in the public annals of his time. But such was the marvellous interest taken in this superlatively gifted man, that religious publications, and publications far from being religious, found it to their interest to publish every fact and incident they could glean concerning his character and work.

I do not, therefore, propose to write another *life* of Mr. Spurgeon. This work will be better left, hereafter, to the one to whom shall be committed the sacred and honourable charge of writing *the life*. He told me years ago that if his life ever must be written he should like Paxton Hood to do it, if that distinguished author survived him. But Paxton Hood has been lost to us some years now. Yet, as Mr. Spurgeon once said in speaking of another matter, 'The Lord hath His servant making ready, and when the time shall come, when the hour shall want the man, the man shall be found for the hour;' so doubtless it will be concerning this pleasant yet responsible task.

I propose writing of Mr. Spurgeon as I knew him, and as I saw him, under a great variety of circumstances and conditions; giving, I trust, no offence in anything, that this ministry be not blamed.

It was, in the good providence of God, my singular fortune and unspeakable joy to be favoured with the close and intimate friendship of Mr. Spurgeon for many years. In his letters, souvenirs, in the tender and affectionate inscriptions in the many choice volumes he gave me, in the many affectionate things he said to me, and, above all, in the priceless influence his spirit exerted over mine, I have precious memorials of his love.

Perhaps it will satisfy the curiosity of some at the outset if I briefly tell how I came to be favoured with the intimacy of one so far above and beyond me in intellect, character, and position. My life touched that of Mr. Spurgeon's in several ways that were exceptional. All who have read any account of his childhood are familiar with the striking incident connected with the Rev. Richard Knill's visit to the house of Mr. Spurgeon's grandfather, the Rev. James Spurgeon, at Stambourne, in Essex. C. H. Spurgeon was then a boy, and was staying with his grandfather. In Mr. Knill's biography it is recorded: 'When walking and conversing with the boy in the garden Mr. Knill became pervaded by a deep concern for him, and, turning aside into an arbour formed by an old yew-tree, he placed his hands upon his head and invoked the Divine blessing upon him, saying at the close that he believed that he would live to love Jesus Christ, and preach His Gospel to the largest congregation in the world.' Richard Knill became minister of Queen Street *Independent* Church, Chester, of which my mother became a member, she having been blessed through the ministry of Mr. Knill. When I was but a few weeks old Mr. Knill 'baptised' me. He took me into his arms, and, dedicating me to God, offered a fervent prayer for my future. These two incidents helped to draw us together. Moreover, my wife was born in the same village as Mr. Spurgeon, Kelvedon, in Essex. Also I had the privilege of becoming a student in his college, and, after a three years' pastorate in the country, of being called to be minister over the Church which is only a few minutes' walk from the Tabernacle. So I settled nearer to him than any of the other students. Moreover, Mrs. Spurgeon's father and mother were members of our Church when it was situated in Church Street, Blackfriars Road. Mr. Spurgeon was singularly interested in the welfare of our Church, and when, after having had a trying interregnum of decline, it became revived and prosperous, he greatly rejoiced, and seemed to give me more and more of his friendship and love.

Living near to the college, I availed myself of the privilege of attending his Friday lectures to his students for fourteen years. Here

Mr. Spurgeon was often seen at his best; and since I took notes on nearly every occasion I find myself in possession of very many of his smart, sententious, and humorous utterances. I often went also to the Thursday Evening Service, when many of his greatest and most masterly discourses were delivered. Added to these advantages of seeing and hearing the gifted lecturer and preacher, I had a standing invitation to his house, of which privilege the reader may be sure I availed myself as often as conscience would allow. Many were the holidays we took together; but of these something will be said further on.

The wit of Mr. Spurgeon was proverbial. Indeed, multitudes who had no idea of his possessing the many other qualities which blended so harmoniously in him, and together made that full-orbed character he possessed, yet knew him as a man who could say some very odd and funny things. As I shall give some samples of his wit, it may not be inappropriate here to say a little concerning this gift-so choice, so rare. Mr. Spurgeon's faculty of humour was doubtless inherited. I was dining some time ago in the hospitable home of Mr. James Doulton, at Wraysbury, with the venerable, and now, alas! deceased, Joshua Harrison, who went to school with Mr. Spurgeon's father and uncle. The saintly man related several incidents connected with their school life, which proved to me that C. H. Spurgeon was not the first of the Spurgeon family in whom the element of fun was particularly strong; while in shrewd business tact they also seemed to exhibit the very practical ability of their famous son and nephew.

What a bubbling fountain of humour Mr. Spurgeon had! I have laughed more, I verily believe, when in his company than during all the rest of my life besides. How versatile and multiform were the shapes, garbs, and postures his wit assumed! Now, it was a pat allusion to some historic character or funny story; or a singular application of a trivial saying; or the forging of an apposite sentence full of playful surprise. Anon, it was a play upon words and phrases, taking advantage of the ambiguity of their sense or the affinity of their sound. Again, it wrapped itself in a humorous expression, or leaped out in an odd similitude, a sly question, a smart answer, a quirkish reason, a shrewd imitation. Sometimes it flashed out in a clever retort, an out-of-the-way objection, a striking hyperbole, a bit of bold irony, in a look or gesture of mimicry, or in a bit of acute nonsense.[1]

As to adequately defining it, one may as well try to make a portrait of the whistling wind or a figure of the fleeting air. The play of his fancy, the flashes of his merriment, the brilliant sparkling of his genius, were as charming in their beauty as they were astonishing in their variety. They ever excited within one both wonder and delight. C. H. Spurgeon had himself the most fascinating gift of laughter I ever knew in any man, and he had also the greatest ability for making all who heard him laugh with him. Did not much of his power for usefulness lie in his bright and sunny disposition? I think one writer speaks wisely and truly when he says: 'The world will never be converted to God until Christians cry less and laugh and sing more. The horrors are a poor bait. If people are to be persuaded to adopt our holy religion, it will be because they have made up their minds that it is a happy religion. They don't like a morbid Christianity. Plant the Rose of Sharon along the church walks, and columbine to clamber over the church walls, and have a smile on the lip, and have the mouth filled with holy laughter. There is no man in the world except the Christian that has the right to feel an untrammelled glee.'

Mr. Spurgeon was as familiar with the glades of grief and the dark narrow gorges of depression as any man, or he could never with such

---

[1] I am indebted to an old author for part of this description of wit.

consummate art have ministered comfort to the suffering, sorrowing sons of men. But none knew better than he what the laughter Divine means of which the Psalmist speaks: 'Then was our mouth filled with laughter,' and which Abraham indulged in when 'he fell upon his face and laughed.' I well remember him telling the students one Friday afternoon a bit of his own experience which will illustrate and prove this. He said: 'Gentlemen, there are many passages of Scripture which you will never understand thoroughly until some trying or singular experience shall interpret them to you. The other evening I was riding home after a heavy day's work; I felt very wearied and sore depressed, when swiftly and suddenly as a lightning flash that text came to me, "My grace is sufficient for thee." I reached home and looked it up in the original, and at last it came to me in this way. "My grace is sufficient for THEE," and I said, "I should think it is, Lord," and burst out laughing. I never fully understood what the holy laughter of Abraham was until then. It seemed to make unbelief so absurd. It was as though some little fish, being very thirsty, was troubled about drinking the river dry, and Father Thames said, "Drink away, little fish, my stream is sufficient for thee." Or it seemed like a little mouse in the granaries of Egypt, after the seven years of plenty, fearing it might die of famine. Joseph might say, "Cheer up, little mouse, my granaries are sufficient for thee." Again, I imagined a man away up yonder on a lofty mountain saying to himself, "I breathe so many cubic feet of air every year, I fear I shall exhaust all the oxygen in the atmosphere;" but the earth might say, "Breathe away, O man, and fill thy lungs ever, my atmosphere is sufficient for thee." Oh, brethren, be great believers! Little faith will bring your souls to heaven, but great faith will bring heaven to your souls.'

It will not be supposed, however, that there was little in his talk besides that which provoked a smile or excited a laugh. Neither the sacred rapture of soul which caused him to laugh as Abraham did, nor yet the innocent merriment of spirit which made his company to be as cheering 'as winter's sun or summer's shade,' was his abiding mood. His normal state was rather one of calm, delightful *restfulness*. Goethe says, 'All great service comes from the centre of a calm heart,' and Mr. Spurgeon was mighty in word and deed because his whole being found repose in God. Both head and heart he rested on his Saviour's bosom. His spirit of humour was, however, so strong that he might as well have tried to silence the echo or chain the lightning as to prevent its disclosing itself. When someone blamed him for saying humorous things in his sermons, he said: 'He would not blame me if he only knew how many of them I keep back.' Yet his speech was even more marked by its sound and sober sense, by its wisdom and terseness, than by its play of fancy and gracious mirthfulness.

He often spoke in proverbs, and had there only been with him from the beginning of his public career some judicious Boswell (despite what Macaulay says) to have noted and preserved his wise, weighty, and witty sentences given in private conversation, and of which he himself thought little or nothing, the Church and the world might have been enriched today by a volume of proverbial philosophy second only in value to the book by Israel's gifted king. When he suspected me of acting the part of a Boswell, he said he thought if I was going to 'Boswellise' him he should be ready to hang me. I told him, however, I had preserved much of what I had heard him say, especially his humorous sayings. He said: 'All right; only let me see them one day.' Happily, many specimens of his short, pithy utterances are preserved to us in his two volumes of *Salt-cellars*. If the reader has not obtained them, let him do so, and many an hour of profitable and pleasant reading will be his reward. But to hear him talk as he there writes, with the twinkling eye and the voice soft and mellow as a silver bell, was a privilege to remember. I hope in the ensuing chapters each reader may participate to some extent in the joy I experienced when in company with one of the master minds and most gracious characters of this or indeed of any age.

CHAPTER II

THE CHARM OF HIS FRIENDSHIP

As with tens of thousands, my first acquaintance with Mr. Spurgeon was through his books. I had not long been awakened to religious concern when I found myself one evening engaged with another youth in a rather animated discussion as to who was England's greatest preacher. Though neither of us knew many - but then we were only boys - my ideal up to that time had been a noted preacher from Liverpool; and for him I claimed the palm.

'Ner-ner-ner-No,' said my opponent, for the poor boy stammered terribly; 'Per-per- spur-Spurgeon's the best.'

'Who's he?' I said, for I did not remember having heard his name.

He gave the information required. My interest in 'this wonderful man' was at once aroused. Soon after this I had put into my hands, by a Christian matron who was anxious for my spiritual well-being, one of his sermons, entitled 'The Power of Christ illustrated by the Resurrection.' It was delivered on January 29, 1871, and is No. 973 in the *Tabernacle Pulpit.* This sermon amazed me. I felt bewildered, and almost stunned by it, and exclaimed, 'The gods are come down to us in the likeness of men!' It gave me a conception of Christ I had not hitherto possessed. It seemed to flood my soul with light divine, and bring to my anxious heart a restful benediction from God. For the first time I saw how sublime were the possibilities of character and service to the man who possessed Christ, and who was possessed by Him.

'There are no ebbs and flows with Christ's power,' says the preacher. 'Omnipotence is in the hand that once was pierced, permanently abiding there. Oh, if we could but rouse it; if we could but bring the Captain of the host to the field again, to fight for His Church, to work by His servants! What marvels should we see, for He is able! We are not straitened in Him; we are straitened in ourselves, if straitened at all.'

God has favoured me with constant blessing in soul winning for twenty years and more; and I feel that no small measure of it I may owe to the influence of that sermon upon my heart and brain.

Next, I obtained *John Ploughman's Talk*. There were some fellows on the farm whom it described to the letter. So at sunny noon or restful even time, when the labourer's task was o'er, I used to read to them about 'the *idle* man' - we all knew him - 'the religious grumbler,' and he was there; while one ill-tempered fellow got quite angry when I read: 'To have a fellow going about the farm as cross with everybody as a bear with a sore head, with a temper as sour as verjuice and as sharp as a razor, looking as surly as a butcher's dog, is a great nuisance.' This was so true to life that Ned, the waggoner, said, "It worn't in the book at all,' and declared I was 'making on it up.'

Little did I then dream that with this gifted preacher and author I should be privileged to enjoy years of close and happy companionship. I mourn to think it past, and often say, *Why*

> Could not the grave forget thee, and lay low
> Some less majestic, less beloved head?

The first time I saw Mr. Spurgeon was on a Thursday evening in June 1872. I had come up to London to see him about entering college. He was in the pulpit, and preached from 'I will hear what God the Lord will speak: for He will speak peace unto His people, and to His saints; but let them not turn again to folly' (Psalm lxxxv. 8). The sermon has not yet been published; but I remember him saying, 'Sin is always folly, and men are fools who indulge in it; but when a man has once been delivered out of it, and turns again to folly, he is a fool with an emphasis.' During the whole sermon there was scarcely any action; and the truth came forth from his heart and mouth like the calm deep flowing of a majestic river.

The next morning I saw him by appointment at his home in Nightingale Lane. He carefully examined my credentials and testimonials, and said: 'The only objection I can see to your coming into college is you are too young; but you will soon get over that; come; and God bless you; and if you should ever need money while in college ask Mr. B--- from me to give you ten pounds for your own pocket.' I left his presence after this first interview with 'limbs as light as air.' There are no mountains or hills about Clapham Common, or they would have broken forth before me into singing; all the trees did seem to clap their hands. I was to be a minister! the dream of my boyhood, the one ambition of my youth! and to be sent forth by the man whom, above all others, I had come to revere and love. How I afterwards saw and heard him in college will be told presently. In the meantime I will recall some of the many golden hours I spent in his company.

A note like the following was usually the welcome intimation that another season of happy fellowship was to be enjoyed:

Nightingale Lane, Balham

DEAR FRIEND, - If it does not rain, be here on Monday at nine, and I will try and go out for a couple of days holiday with you.

Yours heartily,
C. H. SPURGEON

It did not rain, and together we went to Ewell; Mrs. Spurgeon and a lady friend accompanying us thus far. The ladies returned in the carriage, while we took train into Mid-Surrey, where for several days we stayed. Let the reader fancy himself 'in the high court of Nature,' with some shady grove as a palace, the oak, the beech, and the flowery chestnut forming at once a colonnade and a canopy; with ivy and woodbine for its curtains and tapestry; while robin and blackbird, thrush and linnet, as voluntary minstrels, pour forth their music; and, in addition to these delights of sight and sound, to have the presence of one from whose soul there flowed such words of grace and wisdom as few mortals could utter. There will be no wonder then at any exultation of spirit the writer feels as he recalls the many such experiences he once enjoyed. To sit for hours, as I have often done, with C. H. Spurgeon in some shady bower, on a bright summer's day, and to hear him discourse on the wonders and beauties of Nature, on God in history, of His wisdom and love in grace, came as near being heaven on earth as one is likely to experience or entitled to expect.

On such occasions his soul also was often filled with deep calm joy. 'My life seems to me like a fairy dream,' he said to me in one of these delightful seasons. 'I am often both amazed and dazed with its mercies and its love. How good God has been to me! I feel I would rather be the meanest slave in His kitchen than live in the best palace the devil ever built. To be His dog would be infinitely preferable to being the devil's darling.' Then he would give instances of answered prayer, or remarkable cases of conversion through sermons heard or read. Usually we had with us some choice volume - a commentary on some book of the Bible, or on the geography of Surrey; or perhaps on the vegetable kingdom. A chapter or two from these would suggest some profitable subject for dissertation or discussion.

I remember the subject of *inner consciousness as a guide to truth* being once the theme of conversation. He had been having an argument with some gentleman on the question of the future punishment of the wicked. This man believed in the 'larger hope,' and his argument was that his inner consciousness revolted against eternal punishment; and he held the view of the validity of this inner voice as Tennyson expresses it:

> The wish, that of the living whole
> No life may fail beyond the grave,
> Derives it not from what we have
> The likest God within the soul?

Mr. Spurgeon held that, while the law had been once written upon man's heart, and man's inner consciousness was an infallible guide to truth and duty, sin had now robbed him of all this. The standard of infallibility is not now in man, neither is it in any Church or council, but in the Scriptures; and when inner consciousness upon any matter is contrary to the Word of God, we must know it is not God's voice in us, but rather the devil's; for God never contradicts Himself by saying that within a man which is opposed to the declaration of Scripture. Man's nature is not necessarily an 'organised lie,' but it is not to be trusted as a guide to belief as to what God will do or not do. His antagonist had said; 'I will risk it; and if arraigned for my belief before God's bar will tell Him I derived it from what I had the likest Him within my soul.' 'Then the only answer He will give to that will be, "the thunder of His power,"' said Mr. Spurgeon. Then he said; 'You know, Williams, that while I believe in eternal punishment, and must do, or throw away my Bible, I also believe that *God will give to the lost every consideration* consistent with His justice and His love. There is nothing vindictive in Him, nor can there be in His punishment of the ungodly.'

Speaking of Tennyson's *In Memoriam* reminds me of another reference to it in one of our talks. He said; 'The thought of the poem I consider wonderful, but the *poetry* of it very meagre, and some of the thought I cannot agree with. Tennyson says he holds it truth

> That men may rise on stepping-stones
> Of their dead selves to higher things.

My dead self never helped me to rise; it has always tried to drag and keep me down. I owe nothing to my dead self.'

In commenting once on the words 'and grace for grace' he remarked: 'We get grace to reach out to another grace. Each grace becomes a stepping-stone to something better. I do not believe in our rising on the "stepping-stones of our dead selves." They are poor stones; they all lead downwards. The stepping-stones of the living Christ lead upwards.'

The trees seemed to have a peculiar fascination for him. Often when we were driving along country roads or rural lanes he would keep asking me if I knew the names of the trees. Being born and brought up in the country, I knew them nearly all.

'Now I have you,' he once said. 'You cannot tell me what tree that is.'

'An acacia.'

"Right! Go up to the top of the class.'

He seemed as conversant with the structure and peculiarities of trees as if he had studied nothing else. He would admire and talk about them by the hour together; and if he could only see the squirrels playing their sylvan comedies in some bonny beech, he would enjoy the sight to his heart's content. Since I knew of his love for trees I could well understand him once writing: 'Let John Ploughman be buried somewhere under the boughs of a spreading beech, with a green grass mound above him, out of which primroses and daisies shall peep in their season; a quiet shady spot, where leaves fall, and robins play, and the dewdrops gleam in the sunshine. Let the wind blow fresh and free over my grave; and if there must be a line about me, let it be -

> HERE LIES THE BODY OF
> JOHN PLOUGHMAN
> WAITING FOR THE APPEARING OF HIS
> LORD AND SAVIOUR JESUS CHRIST.'

About each and all the trees he had some instructive remark to make or some historic account to give. The oak would suggest 'Gospel Oak,' and 'Emancipation Oak,' and other histories with which its name stands connected. As for the tree itself, it seemed to have more real majesty than all others. It was a world in itself, a miniature globe. Then he would speak of the peculiarities of its leaves, branches, and bark. The beech tree seemed in its every fibre touched with sympathy; if one branch, striking away from the main trunk, seemed ready to break with its own weight, another branch would be seen to have shot under it to act as a support. The horse chestnut, with its pyramids of delicately marked flowers, so beautiful also in the parabolic form of its branches, and the exquisite shaping of its leaves, ever delighted him. 'If you want to distinguish it in winter from the Spanish chestnut,' he· once said, 'you will find on each leaf stem an impression like a horse-shoe with nails.'

I heard him preach one Thursday evening on the text, 'That they might be called trees of righteousness,' in which, with all his power of apt illustration, he showed the appropriateness of the comparison of good men to trees. 'Trees have been landmarks of history,' said he: 'the Tree of knowledge of Good and Evil marks the Fall; the olive marks the assuagement of the Deluge; the Tree of Mamre notes the era of Abraham; and the palms of Elim record the age of Moses. You may divide the ages if you like by memorable trees. So also by good men.' Then he went on to speak of trees as *centres of attraction*, as *marvels of grandeur*, and as *pictures of beauty*, remarking on the last point: 'Nothing more adorns a landscape than its trees ... A tree, symmetrical from its root to its highest branch, awakens in the mind of the tasteful observer high delight. Such is the beauty of the Christian character.'

Not only instruction, but a good deal of fun often marked his talk about the trees. He was very fond of riddles, and he made large numbers himself. He asked me many suggested by the trees. 'What tree is represented when the fire is burnt out?' 'The *ash*!' 'What tree is represented by a ship out of water?' 'The *beech*!' 'What tree does a child of Hebrew parents remind you of?' 'The *juniper* (Jew nipper).' He could keep on thus until nearly every tree had suggested a riddle of some sort. He told me once how he and his 'son Tom' (as he ever called him) had thus been riddling the trees until they seemed to have exhausted the subject, when 'Tom' said: 'Father, here is another. What tree is represented when the Irishman drives his pig along the road?' 'Give it up, Tom.' 'My hog and I,' was the answer. Many were the stories he told me about his boys. Their juvenile wit often amused him. Tom said when but a little fellow he was 'partial to his papa, but marshal to his mamma.' Charley once pleaded for the 'organ-grinder' to be allowed to play on because all his music was by *handle*. The letters Thomas sent home from New Zealand were ever spiced with fun; and many of the 'tit-bits' the father related for my benefit, and I think also for his own enjoyment. Views of Westwood had been sent out to him, and in writing to express his gratitude he said: 'Yes, Westwood is a paradise, and you, dear father, are *Adam*, and dear mother is *Eve*, and I would I were *Able* to be with you.' But as it is recollections of the father and not the sons I am seeking to give, I must desist. I cannot but record, however, the pleasing fact that both the sons should possess so much of the true nobility of their father's character, as well as not a little of his love of mirthfulness and helpful fun.

The subject of *prayer* was one day being discussed. He gave me some remarkable proofs of its reality and power from his own experience. The funds of the Orphanage, College, and other institutions, had often been replenished in the most remarkable ways, in direct and distinct answers to prayer. Once, when the Orphanage funds were low, he and his co-trustees prayed for help, after giving liberally themselves first of all; and within twenty-four hours over eight hundred pounds came in unsolicited except from God. A gentleman had withdrawn a gift of £-- per annum to one of these objects because a certain action of Mr. Spurgeon had not pleased him. A lady travelled from England to Mentone specially to see him, just at the time notice had been given that the gift would cease. She declared it had been laid upon her heart to come and see him and give him a contribution. She handed him just £--; just the money withdrawn. 'My hair seemed almost to stand on end,' said Mr. Spurgeon. 'I felt God to be so awfully near and real. And yet there are plenty of wretched fellows who declare that there is no such thing as answered prayer. The arguments such men use are exactly like the Irishman's, who, when charged with murder and was told a dozen people saw him do it, said, "I can bring fifty people who did not see me do it."'

I told him of one of whom I had recently heard spending three hours on his knees. 'I could not do it,' he replied, 'if my eternity depended on it! Besides, if I go to the bank with a cheque, what do I want loafing about the premises for, when I have got my money? I go to God with a promise, which is in reality a cheque issued by God Himself on the bank of heaven; He cashes it for me, and then I go and use what He has given me, to His glory. This I take to be the true way of praying. The fact is, long prayers are often the result of unbelief. Yet it is possible, without the formal act of kneeling, for the heart to be praying always. I think I can say that seldom many minutes elapse without my heart speaking to God in either prayer or praise.' And everyone who knew him intimately must have felt it was really and indeed so; for in all his humorous moments he was reverent; and, strange to say, in his most solemn moments he was often humorous. He had not two lives, one religious and the other secular; his whole life was one of uniform and irrevocable consecration to God.

He was ever careful to consult God about every detail of his life. When speaking on this matter during one of our drives, I gave him a sample of it which greatly amused him; and as he afterwards gave it to the students I may relate it as a story he told. I had been in the dentist's hands for several weeks, and upon returning to my weekly prayer meeting, as my people supposed, with several new teeth in my mouth, one of our members, a really good but eccentric old fellow, prayed and said: 'Lord, we thank Thee Thou hast brought back our dear pastor, and, now Thou hast given him his new artificial members, bless them to the proclamation of Thy truth.' Mr. Spurgeon laughed until the carriage shook again when I told him this. This same good brother was in a prayer meeting at which I told my people of the marvellous unanimity displayed among all sections of the Church of Christ at a special prayer meeting at the Tabernacle while Mr. Spurgeon was so ill. He afterwards rose to pray, and said: 'Lord, we thank Thee for the unity of which we have just heard. It seems to us as if the time has come when the leopard is lying down with the kid, and the sucking child is playing on the hole of the cock-a-tri-cock-a-tri-cock-a-tri-den.' No, the dear old fellow did not get out 'cockatrice' so well even as my imperfect attempt to report it would indicate.[1] It was not easy to maintain one's gravity under such circumstances. I heard years ago an old man get up at many Tabernacle prayer meetings and pray in such homely and original phrases as to make the pastor cry with laughter. Even the pastor himself (so spontaneous and perennial was his wit) would sometimes unconsciously verge on the humorous in his prayers; but he never lacked pathos and unction, which frequently moved us to tears.

Preachers and preaching naturally formed a frequent theme of conversation. What knowledge he displayed concerning all the great preachers of every age! He seemed to have made himself familiar with the biographies of every man of note who had occupied the French and Swiss, the Greek and Latin and the German, as well as

---

[1] Since I wrote the above this dear man of God has gone to heaven. I miss him sorely.

the English, Scottish, and Welsh pulpits. Augustine, he said, was the quarry from which nearly all of them had dug. His acquaintance with our great English Puritans is known to most who know anything at all about him. Pointing to shelves loaded with the works of these laborious men, he said one day: 'I have preached them all.' Of Beecher he said: 'He is a much bigger man than I am; but I make up for it by giving a great deal more Gospel.' He referred to Samuel Martin of Westminster with great affection, and said how much he enjoyed his sermons. Of Dr. Maclaren he said, among many other kind things: 'What a tower of strength he is to the Evangelical faith!' Of Bishop Ryle he said: 'I think him the best man in the Church of England.' Here are a few other of the opinions he expressed as to preachers. 'Baptist Noel was a good and noble man, but not equal to his predecessor, Harrington Evans, who would have cut up into thirty of him.' 'My belief is that Joseph Irons of Camberwell was the preacher of his day. I greatly profit by his sermons. I have his own copy of them in four volumes; they were given to me by his widow.' 'Robertson of Brighton was a wonderful preacher. He gave utterance to some of the most beautiful thoughts that ever fell from mortal lips. But what a pity they should be allied with so much that is questionable!' 'I don't know any sermons issued from the press of late years that I like so well as Vaughan's of Brighton.' 'Canon Liddon's sermons are masterpieces.' 'Henry Melvill was a Demosthenes among preachers.'

But with all his appreciation of modern preachers and sermons, he impressed me with the fact that the Puritan authors were by far his greater favourites. Manton he seemed to prize as much, if not more, than all. He must have been well acquainted with this author very early in life, for he gave me a large volume of Manton's expositions, which contains the following in beautiful handwriting:

'This valuable commentary was given to me by a poor aged minister in Bexley, Kent, as an acknowledgment of repeated attempts to provide for his urgent necessities by preaching for him in his little chapel. C. H. Spurgeon, 1856. Manton needs no commendation.' This early estimate of Manton's works increased with years, for in 1883 he published a volume of *Illustrations and Meditations; or, Flowers from a Puritan's Garden*; the Puritan's Garden being Manton's exposition of Psalm cxix. In his preface to this volume of illustrations he says he had come to know Manton so well that he could choose him out from among a thousand divines. He speaks of his works as 'a mighty mountain of sound theology,' and declares that 'ministers who do not know Manton need not wonder if they are themselves unknown.'

Jay of Bath was ever a great favourite. He often read a chapter or two from Jay in college, and advised each student to get his works. He said he once heard Jay preach. He seemed to have taken Matthew Henry for his model, and when he heard him he gave Henry's inimitable description of the father receiving the prodigal, occurring in the commentator's exposition of Luke xv. This Mr. Spurgeon repeated in such a way as to make us fancy we had really heard Jay preach. With a voice deep-toned and graciously tender he said: 'When he was yet a great way off his father saw him, here were *eyes* of mercy; he had compassion, here were *bowels* of mercy; and ran, here were *feet* of mercy; and fell on his neck, here were *arms* of mercy; and kissed him, here were *lips* of mercy *it was all mercy!*'

A few years ago a volume by C. H. Waller, M.A., was sent him for review. It charmed him. He preached two of his published sermons from suggestions the book gave him, acknowledging his indebtedness to the author. We often had talks about Mr. Waller's books after this. He lent me one or two. I have since obtained them all, and they have been a gold mine to me; and, what is more pleasing still, I have received at least three sturdy young men into my Church who attributed their conversion to sermons on phases of truth suggested by Waller. I told Mr. Spurgeon this, and it gratified him to think he had introduced me to this suggestive writer.

Mr. Spurgeon's talk was by no means confined to theological authors and their books. On almost every conceivable subject I have heard him at different times express his judgment. To the first 'Home Rule' Bill of 1886 he was particularly averse. He admired Mr. Gladstone both for his great ability and sterling Christian character, but said he disagreed absolutely with his Irish policy. He declared also his belief that the Grocers' Licence Bill, brought in by Mr. Gladstone, was an awful blunder, and had been the occasion of increasing secret drinking to a terrible extent. 'John Bright is a statesman more after my model, but he was far ahead of his time, and wanted to govern the nation as though men were perfect, instead of recognising that while men are such sinners ideal government is impossible.'

Mr. Gladstone gave Mr. Spurgeon a hearty invitation to visit him at Hawarden. He intended doing so, but it never happened.

A book had been sent to Mr. Spurgeon for review in which the miracles of Scripture were assailed, and the record of them pronounced unworthy of credence. He said: 'Not to believe in the possibility of miracles is absurd, that is, if men believe in God at all. For miracles may as much have entered into God's original intent in governing the world as the general uniformity of law. A clock-maker constructs a clock which he intends shall only strike the hour once in seventy years. Sixty-nine years go by, the clock has never yet struck, but when the seventieth arrives it strikes, and people say it is a miracle. Not at all; it entered into the design of the maker that it should so strike. Its striking now is as distinctly in keeping with its make as its not striking at all for sixty-nine years. Just so with miracles. They are not *after-thoughts* with God. They are not, as some say, a bungling attempt to do that by extraordinary means which could not be done by ordinary. They are as really inwrought into God's government, and as beautifully as the constant ebbing and flowing of the tide or the daily rising and setting of the sun.

The subject of the Revised Version of the Bible came up one day in course of conversation. He said he was greatly disappointed with it. It had doubtless many special excellences, and had given, in many instances, the beautiful shades of meaning contained in the original which were not discernible in the Authorised Version, and so was particularly valuable as an aid to the student. But *as a book for the people* it would bear no comparison with the grand version of 1611. 'The English is so faulty,' he said. 'If those learned divines had only had John Bright on their committee, to have made suggestions as to the English words and sentences they should use, they might have given us a far better version.'

'Your speech at Exeter Hall the other evening was, by general consent, one of the best and most powerful you ever delivered," I said to him one day.

'Yes,' he replied, 'I did feel remarkably helped of God, and I think I can tell you why. I was to have spoken a few days before at a meeting convened at the house of --' (mentioning a certain wealthy nobleman), 'and he was appointed chairman of the meeting. He had expressed a desire that Î should be present. He wanted to meet me. I did not know but that this might mean at some time or another considerable help being given to the Orphanage, and perhaps other of our institutions, so I anticipated with some pleasure being at the meeting. But judge my surprise when I learned that the gentleman who was to take the chair at this *religious* meeting one day purposed to run a favourite horse for a big race on the following day. I was bewildered for a while as to what I should do. But I decided I would not go to the meeting, whatever I might lose. I would not compromise myself with the world in any measure, and so I did not go; and God honoured me at Exeter Hall for that bit of careful walking.'

Talking about a Baptist Church where a dispute was going on which threatened a serious division, he said: 'My fear is that they have grieved the Spirit of God away from them, and our system of Church government is the worst possible if He be not with us; though the best possible if He be present, to guide and rule. It was never meant to work without Him, and, in fact, can only bring confusion and disaster if He abide not in our midst.' I asked him the cause of the quarrel, and he said: 'The pastor thought the biggest person in this universe, next to the Almighty, was a Baptist minister; a deacon did not agree with him, and thought a deacon was; so they had a row.'

After giving God thanks one day for recovery from sickness he said: 'You know all healing power is from God; whatever healing properties there may be in vegetable or mineral substances, He, with gracious forethought, put them there; while the ability rightly to use them is equally His gift. I like what a French surgeon had sculptured over his college gate: "I dressed the wounds, and God healed him."'

'I have been urged to preach on teetotalism,' he once said, 'but I lay the axe at the root of the tree.' Yet in the latter part of his ministry he did, more than in the earlier periods, strongly denounce the drinking customs of the day. He became an abstainer himself, and his attitude towards total abstinence during the last few years of his life was very different from what it was when I first knew him. I remember, when in college, the then vexed question of unfermented wine at the Lord's table was alluded to by him, and he said: 'If my Church do anything to interfere with either of the ordinances as they were observed when I accepted the pastorate, my relationship to the Church is at once changed. I could not sanction it.' But years afterwards he did sanction it; for unfermented wine was introduced by himself, though one of the deacons, since deceased, who was greatly troubled by the change, told me that he took a bottle of the unfermented wine used to a City analyst, and he found 19 percent of alcohol in it. I am sure, however, that is not the case now.

We reached an hotel, where we were once staying, after a long drive; he was very thirsty, and someone said to him: 'Now, would you not like a glass of beer, sir?'

'Yes, I should very much,' he replied.

'Then why not have it? Do you think it would be wrong?'

'No, not wrong, but some poor beggar to whom drink is a temptation might hear of it, and feel encouraged to take a dozen glasses. I abstain for the sake of such.'

We were sitting at a railway station waiting for our train. He began reading the advertisements on the walls, and many funny things he said about some of them. Then he saw a notice of some special whisky recommended as being *elixir vitae*. 'The elixir of life!' he said; 'ugh! death and damnation! - that's what that is.'

John B. Gough, the great temperance reformer, and he were much attached to each other for several years before the renowned platform orator died. Soon after Mr. Spurgeon first came to London, Mr. Gough gave several of his famous lectures in Exeter Hall. Mr. Spurgeon heard him there, and I have heard him describe with evident delight the marvellous dramatic power that characterised the delivery. One piece of acting greatly impressed him when the lecturer, taking the whole length of the platform, illustrated a man walking up Mount Etna *knee deep in burning lava.* 'It was so powerfully realistic,' said Mr. Spurgeon, 'that I felt the hot ashes up to my knees.' Several years after a temperance organisation had been formed at the Tabernacle, I asked him if more had joined the Church since its inauguration than before; he said, 'No, I cannot say we have had more, but I believe in it for all that.' Speaking at one of the Tabernacle temperance meetings he humorously said: 'All the strongest things drink water - lions, tigers, elephants, and steam engines.'

The only Saturday afternoon I ever knew Mr. Spurgeon to be out when I went to see him was when he took Mr. Gough to see the Orphanage. On that Saturday the touching incident occurred of which Mr. Gough made such use, and which he narrates in his book, *Sunlight and Shadow*, and as this is so thoroughly characteristic, we reproduce it here. After escorting Mr. Gough over the Orphanage Mr. Spurgeon said:

"'Will you go to the infirmary? We have an infirmary and quarantine; for sometimes the poor creatures we take in need a good deal of purifying. We have one boy very ill with consumption; he cannot live, and I wish to see him, for he would be disappointed if he knew I had been here and had not seen him."

'We went into the cool and sweet chamber and there lay the boy. He was very much excited when he saw Mr. Spurgeon. The great preacher sat by his side, and I cannot describe the scene. Holding the boy's hand in his, he said: "Well, my dear, you have some precious promises in sight all around the room. Now, dear, you are going to die, and you are very tired of lying here, and soon you will be free from all pain, and you will rest. Nurse, did he rest last night?" "He coughed very much." "Ah, my dear boy, it seems very hard for you to lie here all day in pain, and cough all night. Do you love Jesus?" "Yes." "Jesus loves you. He bought you with His precious blood and He knows what is best for you. It seems hard for you to lie here and listen to the shouts of the healthy boys outside at play. But soon Jesus will take you home, and then He will tell you the reason, and you will be so glad." Then, laying his hand on the boy, without the formality of kneeling, he said, "O Jesus, Master, this dear child is reaching out his thin hand to find Thine. Touch him, dear Saviour, with Thy loving, warm clasp. Lift him as he passes the cold river, that his feet be not chilled by the water of death; take him home in Thine own good time. Comfort and cherish him till that good time comes. Show him Thyself as he lies here, and let him see Thee and know Thee more and more as his loving Saviour." After a moment's pause he said: "Now, dear, is there anything you would like ? Would you like a little canary in a cage to hear him sing in the morning? Nurse, see that he has a canary tomorrow morning. Good-bye, my dear; you will see the Saviour perhaps before I shall."

'I had seen Mr. Spurgeon holding by his power sixty five hundred persons in a breathless interest; I knew him as a great man universally esteemed and beloved; but as he sat by the bedside of a dying pauper child, whom his beneficence had rescued, he was to me a greater and grander man than when swaying the mighty multitude at his will.'

Like many public men, Mr. Spurgeon had to exercise instant vigilance against impositions by begging impostors. He has told the world himself how he has been taken in more than once. But he told me a singular circumstance that happened to him. A smart, well dressed young fellow called at Westwood, and introduced himself as Henry Ward Beecher's son. Mr. Spurgeon saw him and took him for a walk round the garden. He brought, he said, his father's esteem and affection to him, and told quite a number of stories, all imaginary, about Mr. Beecher's family and Church. Eventually Mr. Spurgeon said he must bid him good-bye, when the young man said, 'Oh, Mr. Spurgeon, would you oblige me by cashing a cheque for me?' His suspicion was immediately aroused, and he said, 'No, I cannot; and I don't think you ought to ask, or expect me to do so. You are a perfect stranger to me. If you are Mr. Beecher's son you have with you, surely, sufficient credentials to enable you to get change at the right quarter.' The pseudo-Beecher quickly left him. A few days after this happened a terrible murder was committed on the London and Brighton Railway. An elderly gentleman met his death in a first-class carriage at the hands of a young man named Lefroy, who was subsequently captured. His portrait appeared in the illustrated papers. Mr. Spurgeon saw it, and at once recognised it as that of the young man who had called on him as Mr. Beecher's son.

He was not always so fortunate in escaping imposition. A man called at the Tabernacle once to see him; he 'was told Mr. Spurgeon was at home. He was collecting for some noble object, and wanted to enlist Mr. Spurgeon's practical sympathy. Mr. Spurgeon's brother was told about the matter shortly after the man had left the Tabernacle. From the description given he recognised him as an impostor. He either went, or sent a messenger immediately to his brother; but it was too late; the man had called and obtained 10*l*., so specious and apparently genuine were his claims. When Mr. Spurgeon discovered that he had been done he said: 'Dear me: I did not think human nature could have sunk so low.'

Yet he never allowed such unfortunate incidents to interrupt the flow of his splendid generosity. He was always and ever giving. He put 20*l*. into my hands one day to give to a poor minister who was in great trouble and was rather pinched in his circumstances. On an anniversary occasion he was to have preached for me. On the day appointed for the service a terrible snowstorm came. He could not come, but sent me the following letter with a 10*l*. note in it - but about this he says nothing:

> Westwood, Beulah Hill, Upper Norwood: March 17
>
> DEAR MR. WILLIAMS, - I could not get down from these Alps on Tuesday. We were snowed up, and no horse could do the journey. I was greatly vexed, but I could not walk. My soul could neither fly nor go, but I was like a caged bird. What shall I do to make a recompense? I am at your disposal for a service whenever I can hold it, and it will suit you. Today is better for locomotion, and it does not snow, and so I hope to venture out. If I were but stronger I should not be such an unprofitable servant to those who seek my help. The Lord bless you evermore.
>
> Yours ever heartily,
>
> C. H. SPURGEON

His heart was so full of generous affection that he seemed to be ever devising some new way of expressing it; and it shall be known in *that day* to how many hundreds his generous soul overflowed in deeds of kindness, too sacred to be yet told. He was as princely in his giving as he was in his preaching.

So many of his sayings, his references to events, to men, to books, to conditions and circumstances, occur to me as I write that I must ask the reader to allow me to give a few of them as they come.

'Is your gout hereditary, sir?' I said one day when he was suffering from this painful malady. 'I hope in God's name it is not,' he responded. 'If it is, I could almost wish I were never married, for I would rather endure almost anything than give it even to a dog.'

'Shall I ever get over my terrible nervousness before going into the pulpit?' I asked. 'If ever you do, all your power will be gone,' was his quick response. 'I suffer from it, and always have done, as no tongue can tell.'

'Tell me about your courting, Williams,' he said. 'I should like to know its origin and history. Where did you find your wife? What did you say to her? Just tell me.' 'All that has been forgotten through the bliss that has succeeded,' I said. 'There, I won't ask you to tell me anything more, for you cannot improve on that little speech all day,' was his playful response. The first time he met my wife he said to me, 'Ah! Williams, now I know the secret of all the good I have found in you.' Driving behind a pair of horses with a friend of his and mine once, who was then unmarried, he said to him, 'Look at those horses: they both pull different ways; mind what sort of a wife you get.'

I spoke once of a letter I had just received from some unknown man who had heard me preach, and had profited by the sermon, but who reproached me for not coming down among the people afterwards and speaking personally to them. He said my earnestness was simulated, or I would have done that. 'There will only be one bigger fool than that man, and that will be you if you take any notice of him,' he exclaimed. 'As well blame the Queen if she gave 100 lbs. of butter to the poor, for not spreading it on their bread'

'What are you going to preach from tomorrow?' he once asked me. '"The curse of the Lord is in the house of the wicked, but He blesseth the habitation of the just."' He gave a deep sigh; his countenance changed even before I had finished the verse, brief as it was; and he said in tones of deep solemnity, '*Ah, me!*' 'What is the matter, sir?' 'Don't you know,' he replied, 'that is the text I had on that terrible night of the accident at the Surrey Music Hall?' I did not know it, but I learned from the mere mention of it how permanent was the effect upon his mind of that awful night's disaster. I never alluded either to this text or to the Surrey Gardens calamity after that. I cannot but think, from what I saw, that his comparatively early death might be in some measure due to the furnace of mental suffering he endured on and after that fearful night.

Mr. Spurgeon did not allude often to his own books; yet at times he would speak of letters he had received expressing gratitude for the blessing they had been. *The Clue of the Maze* he talked out to Mr. Harrald under the trees in a garden at Mentone, and it seemed to give him pleasure to rehearse its arguments. I told him I thought *According to Promise* and *All of Grace* two of the best books he ever wrote. He did not assent to this, but was glad that testimonies to their usefulness had been so abundant. I expressed the opinion that the earlier volumes of his *Treasury of David* were not equal to the later ones. Mrs. Spurgeon, who was present, dissented from this; but he concurred, and added: 'I could much improve those earlier volumes if I went over them again.' When he was expounding for the *Treasury* Psalm cxix. he said: 'It is no easy task, for the thought gets thinner as I get near the end.' I had an idea that he meant the thought in the Psalm, but have since concluded he meant his own thought; for as the Psalm has all through a sameness of subject, and even of expression, notwithstanding its variety, he found it 'no easy task' to preserve a freshness of expository thought on to the end. Yet he did so.

I ventured to say to him that while his exposition of Psalm cxxxvii. in the *Treasury* was exceedingly good, yet the exposition he gave of it in public once was even better. 'Why did you not print that?' I said. He did not remember having expounded it, or he would have asked if it was in manuscript. 'Can you tell me anything of it?' he said. 'Yes, I can.' I gave it to him. 'What a memory you have!' he said 'I never knew anyone with a better. You ought to be thankful it is allied with other abilities, for while memory is exceedingly useful as an auxiliary talent, it is, in and of itself, the least of all talents, and is a gift we have in common with lower orders of creation. A horse has memory; a dog memory; an elephant memory; even a tree has memory, for if you cut its bark it will retain the impression for years.'

Allusion was made in our conversation one day to the singular application of the text to his mind when he was seeking to go to college, 'Seekest thou great things for thyself? Seek them not,' which seemed to have changed the current of his career. I told him that soon after I came into college I began to suffer from deep depression of spirit, occasioned by the sudden change from an active life in the country to the sedentary life of study in the classrooms beneath the Tabernacle. The present college was not then built. I was ready to give up all idea of the ministry in sheer despair, when one day in the interval between the classes I went alone into the Tabernacle pulpit, and looked round in admiration and astonishment at the magnificent building. When, as distinctly to me as any voice I ever heard, someone said, 'You will preach here one day,' I turned round to see 'the voice that spake with me,' but no other person was in the building. I felt assured then, and do still, that God did thus speak. I told no one at the time, but I was greatly cheered by the assurance given that I should yet be able to preach with sufficient acceptance to preach there. It was not until I had occupied the Tabernacle pulpit a number of times that I ventured to speak to Mr. Spurgeon of this, to me, real, though singular, experience. He bowed his head and said, 'Yes; I do believe God does thus speak to men sometimes.'

When his heart began to be greatly troubled concerning the state of religious thought in the Churches, he commenced writing his volume entitled *Cheque Book of the Bank of Faith*. In the preface to this choice book he says: 'I commenced these daily portions when I was wading in the surf of controversy." To those of us who were permitted to have intercourse with him, the spirit and matter of this book were indicated in several ways long before the book itself was written. At home his readings were more often than usual out of the Book of Jeremiah; for with this prophet he seemed, more than with all others, to have just then a deep sympathy and experimental acquaintance. I heard another leading minister say, at the time of the 'Down-Grade' controversy, that Jeremiah was to him then what he had never been before. His pulpit utterances, too, about that time were charged with a spirit of jealous solicitude, lest the very men who were ostensibly set for the defence of the Gospel should prove untrue to their sacred trust.

I am not, however, intending to introduce the 'Down-Grade' controversy here; but I speak of this *Cheque Book* more especially to note a rather singular experience connected with it, and which I told Mr. Spurgeon, to his evident enjoyment and delight. It may seem strange to the reader, but it is not more strange than true. I said to Mr. Spurgeon - one Saturday, I think it was: 'I have had a singular experience, sir, in connection with your volume, *The Cheque Book of the Bank of Faith*.' 'Tell me what it is,' he replied. 'Well, there was until lately, in a garden opposite my study, a large retriever dog; he barked incessantly almost day and night, until I found study to be out of the question. An appeal to the owner brought the reply: "I cannot help the dog barking; I am not going to trouble about him."' Trivial as it may seem, the matter was one of great moment to me.

What was I to do? Then the thought occurred, 'Pray about it.' I rather smiled at the idea, and said to myself, 'It may after all only be a nervous fad; you cannot surely go to God about a matter like this.' I was reading just at that time, day by day, *The Cheque Book of the Bank of Faith*, taking a chapter each morning. A day or two after I had received the message from the owner of the dog I came to the portion for June 5. My mind was at the same time really disturbed and troubled about this dog nuisance. Well, I opened the book for my morning portion, June 5. Judge of my surprise when I read the text for the day: 'But against any of the children of Israel shall not a dog move his tongue.' But let the reader imagine my still greater surprise when the comment on the text was read. It began as follows: 'What! has God power over the tongues of dogs? Can He keep curs from barking? Yes, it is even so.' I could read no further just then, for no bulldog ever laid hold with greater tenacity than this text, and the comment on it, did on me. I there and then fell on my knees and asked God to stop this nuisance; and I had rest about the matter as soon as I rose from my knees. Now, let the reader note. Within a fortnight - I think within a week - the dog and the whole family left the house. I made inquiries about this sudden move, and found that the owner of the dog had seen another house he took a fancy to, and had decided to move at once. I write this in the study in which that singular text was read and that simple prayer offered. A new tenant occupies the house, who seems to be particularly fond of dogs, for I often see three or four running about his garden. Yet I have never, for one five minutes, been disturbed by his dogs barking. Can I ever say No to these questions: 'What! has God power over the tongues of dogs? Can He keep curs from barking?' I need scarcely say that this story quite laid hold of the author of *The Cheque Book*, and greatly amused and cheered him.

He was exceedingly low and depressed in spirits one day when we were together. I never knew him but on this occasion to hint a doubt as to his own standing in Christ. He did not actually do so then, but said such a sense of utter unworthiness came over him sometimes as to make him dread being numbered among the unprofitable servants. I said: 'I will risk my eternal welfare upon the same foundation upon which you are resting, sir.' 'Don't you be a fool, Williams,' he replied; 'trust in the Lord Jesus for yourself, and you are safe; but never trust upon the trust of another. Christ is absolutely to be trusted, but we can never say the same of any mortal man's experience. Nevertheless, I do trust Him. He is my only hope.'

Soon after I came to London my own place of worship was being renovated, and I preached for several Sundays in the large hall of the college. I met him one week day during this period, and he said: 'Oh, Williams, the sight of you explains a mystery. I thought it was a terrible thunder-clap I heard while preaching on Sunday, but I forgot you were preaching in the college; that accounts for it.' 'Yes,' said a minister standing by, 'he is a Boanerges, is he not?' 'I don't know about that,' said Mr. Spurgeon, 'I only know he is a Barnabas to me.' 'What a *wooden* lot of ministers Upton has had!' he once playfully remarked. 'There was Mr. Cole, and Bigwood, and Branch, and Barker; but they were all good men and true.'

'I was seeing inquirers for four hours yesterday,' he told me one day. 'It was glorious work.' Then he went on to describe some of the thirty-four cases he had dealt with. Some of them were specially remarkable; and the testimony they gave him of blessing received through his sermons was as the dew of the Lord to his spirit. No man ever possessed more of 'instinct for souls' than he. He once showed me a letter written, I believe, by some poor woman in the backwoods of America. The writing was the most curious I ever saw. It had puzzled him for hours before he could decipher it; but he discovered it was a letter of gratitude for a sermon of his that had found its way to that 'out of the world' region, and which had led this poor woman to the Saviour. 'This is more precious to me than a big bank note," he said with tears in his eyes,

Mr. Spurgeon once told me the following incident: 'A gentleman came one day to look over the Pastors' College. He said to me, "And you mean to tell me all this money is sent you in answer to prayer; I don't believe it." I said, "I don't ask you to believe it." He said, "Oh no! good people know you are a good manager, and they send you the money." My reply was, "If good people had not got the money, God would send the devil with it." After we had looked the place over he said, "Well, it is a capital institution; here is ten pounds for you." I thanked him. "But," I said, "you told me *good* people sent me the money I hope that applies to you." "Oh no," he said, "you hit me very hard when you said He would send the devil with it." And so he went away, for he was a fast-living sort of man.'

'What books are you reading now?' he asked me one day. 'Carlyle's *French Revolution*,' I said. 'Very good; it is a fine work, full of nervous, bracing thought and stirring facts, but I think it cannot be appreciated at its true worth unless simpler histories of France have been read before beginning it. I would not advise anyone to take Carlyle as a first study. Scott's *Life of Napoleon* is a good history. That first Napoleon was a really great man. He had a mind, and no mistake; his successors have been insignificant in comparison.' 'You like Boswell's *Johnson*, sir, of course.' 'Oh yes; that is the biography, it stands unrivalled, and probably ever will; and I think Lockhart's *Life of Scott* and Mrs. Oliphant's *Life of Edward Irving* come next. Sir Walter Scott had probably the greatest mind God ever created; he was indeed the Wizard of the North. How marvellous his stories are! You've not read *Pickwick*, Williams?' 'No, I have not yet.' 'Oh dear; I was going to say I wish I had not, for I should like once more to enjoy it as I did at the first reading. You have a treat in store. The humour of it is about perfect.'

The Story of the Nations series greatly interested him. He read *Egypt* through at least three times, and eagerly took up the others as they came out. It was exceedingly entertaining and instructive to hear him talk about the people and countries with which the volumes deal. He wrote when reviewing a volume of the series on Carthage;

'No reader of fiction can have been more absorbed in his author's day-dreams than we have been in these veritable records of actual history. He cannot have been profited even to a fractional part of our profiting.' The *History of Ireland* excited his interest and curiosity. He repeated to me the notice he had written on the book, but as his review is printed I take a line or two from that. 'Of all the *Stories of the Nations*, this must be hardest to tell. Like the tale of *The Poor Needy Knife-grinder*, there is no story at all. All the tragedies are comical, and all the comedies are tragical. The road through Irish history is made up of lanes which wind about, and never come to an end till they twist into pathways which never begin. When a man conquers he becomes a victim, and when he is beaten he goes on beating someone else. Ireland has never been at peace except during a great war, and it has never been united except in the agreement to divide, and upon that it was never of one mind.'

Some years ago a good brother used occasionally to speak at meetings attended by Mr. Spurgeon, who was greatly amused by his evident consciousness of his own worth. 'Didn't you notice his motto, Williams, *"I for one! I for one?"* I begin to think a report I got of a sermon he once preached is correct. I asked a gentleman who heard him what he had said, and he replied, "I have a full report of the sermon in my pocket; I will give it you;" and he took out a piece of paper with nothing on it but a big "I." What a pity the man should not be a little more humble! He would be much more useful.' I spoke to him about a certain Grecian philosopher, and in pronouncing his name laid the accent on the wrong syllable. He corrected me, saying, 'The accent is on the other syllable.' I said, 'How was I to know that, sir?' 'Ah! that gives me a thought,' he replied. The next week he gave in college a most fascinating lecture on the pronunciation of words, English and foreign, and spoke of certain guiding principles, which have doubtless been a help to many a student since.

'An amusing incident occurred the other day,' he said once. 'I was dining with Mr. --, and a foreign Rabbi was present. Hot ducks were part of the fare, of which the Rabbi was not allowed to partake, a duck having webbed feet. He gave two or three significant sniffs, and got in that way as much of the ducks as he dare, and turning to me said, *"Moses very hard, Moses very hard."* " Yes," I said, "there is a yoke upon the neck which neither your fathers nor ye have been able to bear."'

We were talking one day about philanthropic institutions. He said there were two ways of maintaining them; by implicit and absolute reliance upon God, or by looking to man. 'Some seem to think there is a *via media*, and that it is well to look to both, in case God fails; but it never succeeds. I had Mr. -- to see me one day, and, as you know, he is the head of a philanthropic movement. He was greatly troubled because they were getting deeply into debt, and funds were coming in very slowly. I told him I could scarcely wonder at it, for he had been doing his best to secure the patronage of this noble personage and the other, and failing to trust in God as he should. To all who act so God says: "If I am not enough, depend upon the great and wealthy among men, and see if they prove sufficient for you; but I cannot help such as try to rest one foot on Me and one on their fellows." Look at Mr. Muller's great work and Miss Sharman's; they look to God absolutely, and He supplies their needs. We do so for funds for our Orphanage, and He has never failed us yet. There is a legitimate use of means made in dependence on God; but this is very different from relying on the great and wealthy among men.'

He went to look over some new premises erected for religious purposes by an ardent believer in the speedy return of our Lord. 'How long a lease did you say you had on these premises?' inquired Mr. Spurgeon. 'Twenty-five years,' was the reply. 'Don't you think it was very unwise to spend all this money on these buildings when you have only twenty-five years' lease?' 'Oh! the Lord will come before then.' 'Well,' said Mr. Spurgeon, 'if I had done it, I should be afraid that when the Lord did come He would want to know what I had been doing not to make better use of His money.'

He greatly admired Mr. Moody and his work. I drove with him from Westwood to Croydon once when he preached for Mr. Moody to a great concourse of people in the hall specially erected for his evangelistic meetings. The intensity of Mr. Moody's spirit greatly charmed him. He said he was the only man who could say the word *Mesopotamia* in two syllables.

He told one man his conscience must be a new one, for he never seemed to use it.

I heard Mr. Spurgeon once introduce a man of rather short stature, who made up for any lack of height by the rotundity of his frame, to the meeting at which he was to speak, as 'this terrestrial ball,' greatly to the amusement of the gentleman himself as well as the people.

During a session of the Congregational Union in London, Mr. Spurgeon went to speak at one of the meetings. He came in late, having had another meeting. He narrated his experience of the evening to me with no small measure of delight. The building was crowded to suffocation, and on the platform were many ministers and laymen of eminence. When his advent was noticed, there was for a few minutes a general hubbub. The gentleman who was speaking soon brought his speech to a close, and one of the officials on the platform fixed *suddenly* on a hymn, and gave it out. Strange to say, as the congregation proceeded with the singing, it was discovered that the hymn was one to be used for an infant baptismal service. Samuel Morley was sitting next to Mr. Spurgeon. Mr. Spurgeon whispered to him, 'How is Mrs. Morley getting on?' 'Getting on?' said Mr. Morley; 'she is quite well.' 'How is the baby? alive and well, I trust,' said Mr. Spurgeon. By the time this brief conversation was concluded both Mr. Morley and the audience saw what a blunder had been made in the hymn chosen and laughter rather than singing seemed to be for the moment the exercise of each one. 'The baptismal hymn' concluded, Mr. Spurgeon rose to speak. Great fun was created when he repeated what he had said in a whisper to Mr. Morley, and when he added how greatly disappointed he felt at not having witnessed the very interesting ceremony the hymn chosen had led him to expect.

He went to preach at Southampton, and was the guest of the Dean. He gave me a long and interesting account of this visit. Lord Radstock was there, and several clergymen and curates of the High Church School. A discussion was started by one of the clergy on the question of the 'Sacraments,' and on baptism in particular. I cannot remember all Mr. Spurgeon told me, but he said: 'Lord Radstock sat *there*, the Dean *there*, Mr. -- there, and Mackey on a hassock near my feet. One of the company said to me, "Now, Mr. Spurgeon, you will grant that our Lord instituted two *Sacraments*, won't you?" "I will grant nothing of the kind," said I; "the Lord Jesus instituted two *ordinances*, which is a very different matter. A sacrament was an oath of allegiance taken by a Roman soldier to the emperor. The Prayer-book may use the term *sacraments*, but the Bible does not, neither will I."' The word *ordinance* was allowed, as expressing more accurately the import of the two commands relating to baptism and the Lord's Supper. The discussion was proceeded with until the question of baptism brought up the vexed subject of 'baptismal regeneration.' All the shot and shell available were brought into requisition to support the High Church view, when Lord Radstock interposed, saying, 'What sort of persons do these become whom you regenerate in baptism? I will tell you. "Eyes have they, but they see not; ears have they, but they hear not; noses have they, but they smell not, neither speak they through their throats. They that make them are like unto them, so is everyone that trusteth in them."' Mr. Spurgeon was greatly delighted with this, in his judgment, singularly apt quotation. He came home and directed his attention to the study of a portion of Romans vi., a passage which Lord Radstock had expounded in the discussion with much ability. Soon after he preached from verses 3 and 4 of this chapter. The sermon is printed in Vol. xxvii., and is singularly full of instruction concerning the believer's union with Christ, as set forth in the Ordinance of Baptism. In the earlier part of this year, 1881, while resting at Mentone, he went carefully through the Epistle to the Romans, and the result was several discourses afterwards upon this instructive book. He spoke to me of the joy and help he had found in the study. He expounded the whole of the Gospel of John at prayers during one Mentone visit.

I heard him once preach in Brunswick Chapel, Leeds. The building belonged to the Methodists, but was lent for the occasion of the Baptist Union meetings. There were many Methodists present at this service. The chapter read was Romans x. The reading, as usual, was accompanied with terse, homely, and suggestive comments. When Mr. Spurgeon reached the thirteenth verse - 'For whosoever shall call on the name of the Lord shall be saved' - he remarked, 'Dear me! How wonderfully like John Wesley the apostle talked! *Whosoever* shall call! *Whosoever!* Why, that is a Methodist word, is it not?' 'Glory! Glory! Hallelujah!' was heard in all parts of the great building. The preacher paused significantly, and proceeded: 'Yes, dear brother, but you read the ninth chapter of this epistle, and see how wonderfully like John Calvin he talked - "That the purpose of God according to election might stand."' There was no 'Glory!' or 'Hallelujah!' following this remark, but many a face was lit up with a significant smile. 'The fact is,' Mr. Spurgeon added, 'that the whole of truth is neither here nor there, neither with this system nor that; neither with this man nor that. Be it ours to know that which is Scriptural in all systems, and to receive it.' The sermon which followed was from I Cor. i. 23: 'But we preach Christ crucified.' I had heard it given in the college a week or so before. It was one of remarkable power. As he preached it at Leeds, he pleaded for simplicity in preaching, and for letting the great theme of 'Christ crucified' speak for itself.

James Wells, of the Surrey Tabernacle, and he did not often meet each other. Mr. Wells considered him far from orthodox, and in preaching once referred to the Tabernacle as 'that mixture-shop over the way.' But nearly all the eminent ministers who differed from Mr. Wells became, at one time or another, the objects of his sarcasm or censure. He referred to Surrey Chapel, when James Sherman preached there, as 'only a dovecot; if you were to go there any time, you would hear little but the cooing of the dove-do, do, do-as though that were the Gospel.'[1] Mr. Spurgeon met Mr. Wells outside the Newington Tabernacle one day, and said he should like to look over the Surrey Tabernacle. Mr. Wells said he would show him over with pleasure, if he would only come on a Monday morning, so that they might have time to fumigate it and purge away any taint of Arminianism that might be left before the next Sunday. This, of course, was fun. Then, Mr. Wells added: 'I did look over your Tabernacle on Saturday.' 'Oh! we shall know how to account, then, for any perfume we may have!' playfully replied the pastor. But the two men had not very much in common, though Mr. Spurgeon did pay Mr. Wells a brotherly visit during his last lingering illness.

I could not but admire a remark he once made to me. We had been speaking about a well-known minister. I said: 'I do not feel much drawn to him, he is so very patronising to me, and seems to try and make me feel how much superior he is. You never do that, sir; why should he?' 'Ah! well,' he replied, 'you must try and think well of him, for he deserves it, and excuse him on the ground of his being so much older than you, if upon no other.'

This readiness to excuse the failings of Christian men was a characteristic of his nature. Many times I had proofs of it. Against hypocrisy, meanness, and deliberate sin, he would hurl thunderbolts of indignation and denunciation; yet he was ever tender toward the frail and weak. He told me once of a student who had 'slipped,' and whom he felt obliged to severely reprimand. ''But,' he said, 'I felt all the time that if I had been in the same circumstances I might have done the same thing, and in my heart I was deeply sorry for him. I trust and believe he will be all right in the future, for he was partly the victim of the stupidity of those who ought to have known better.'

---

[1] Upon another occasion he said: 'Jemmy of the round house never preached a Gospel sermon in all his life;' Surrey Chapel, as most know, being a large circular building. When William Jay preached Rowland Hill's funeral sermon in Surrey Chapel, Mr. Wells spoke of the service from his pulpit as 'a big Jay chattering upon a little Hill.'

CHAPTER III

SUNNY MEMORIES

MR. SPURGEON gave me to understand once and again that I should be welcome at his house any Saturday afternoon I liked to go; but in addition to this privilege I ever and anon received kind little notes or letters from him requesting me to see him on other days, or to be prepared to go out for a day's driving into the country, or, what was more delightful still, to spend a short holiday with him. Many times he pressed me to go with him to Mentone; always expressing his desire several months in advance, that I might have an opportunity of securing supplies for my own pulpit. I deeply regret that I never went, but I fully intended doing so if spared. Alas! the opportunity has gone for ever. I received many Christmas and New Year's cards from him, and always with some word of affection in his own handwriting. I give one only:

With warmest love of
C. H. SPURGEON
Menton, Dec. 22.
Faint yet pursuing

Westwood
Beulah Hill
Upper Norwood.
Jan 21 1881

Dear Friend,

Harrald will be away tomorrow & I shall be all alone — not over bright. Can you leave the queen at the Crown, the circle at the Oval, & come & see one who is ill on the hill, & w[ill] be glad to see you. Yours truly,

C.H. Spurgeon

My reasons for not responding to his repeated request to accompany him on his annual holiday were that I was enjoying perfect health; while the nature of my work was such as to demand, especially in winter time, all my energies and constant presence.

Though I deeply regret that I never visited Mentone with him, I have much to excite my gratitude respecting the hours, days, and weeks we spent together for a series of years at Westwood, in lovely Surrey, at English watering-places, and best of all in 'bonny Scotland.' I am thankful also that the memory of these sacred and privileged seasons so abides with me as to constantly add brightness to my present hours, and to afford me the joy of bringing, as I hope to do, at least a little real felicity and pleasure into the lives of my readers.

On the opposite page is a facsimile of a characteristic note he once sent me. It is necessary to explain that I was living when I received it at '*Crown* Villas, Kennington *Oval.*'

Wednesday was usually his day of rest, and when he could make it convenient, and the weather was agreeable, he would go out into the country driving. He once wrote me: 'As soon as Wednesdays get a little warmer I want you to go out with me. Are you disengaged? - Yours ever lovingly, C. H. SPURGEON.' Upon one occasion, when we had arranged for a day together, I had the following card:

Westwood

DEAR MR. WILLIAMS, - To my great joy my dear wife hopes to go out a little way with me, and so I must forego my choice friend, and neither he nor I will regret it How about the following Wednesday?

Yours heartily,

C. H. SPURGEON

Admitted as I was, for years, to the inner circle of Mr. Spurgeon's home life, it would ill become me to write half a sentence that would betray the confidence thus reposed. But some matters can be spoken of to which neither the departed husband nor his sorely bereaved widow would offer any objection. The home life at Westwood can be described only by the one word beautiful. Mr. Spurgeon loved his wife with a tenderness and intensity of affection I have seldom known equalled, and never excelled; while the devotion of Mrs. Spurgeon to her husband, and her absolute oneness of spirit with him in all his great and holy service, were as nearly perfect as any mortal woman could ever experience or express. Mrs. Spurgeon suffered greatly during all the years I visited the home. The dear man would often speak to me about her sufferings as we were walking round the grounds or were seated in an arbour. His words were too sacred to be repeated; but the patient and even exultant resignation of her spirit to the will of God deeply touched him; while I was, I think, as deeply affected by the resignation he also manifested. 'In all her affliction he was afflicted,' is a text that may, without irreverence, be applied to his own experiences. Yet, as the suffering wife trusted and murmured not, so was it with him. One of the many lessons I learned at Westwood was that grace can indeed teach us 'to suffer and yet be strong;' to be strong in affection to the Father who may sorely chasten us - strong in devotion to the Saviour who for loving and wise purposes brands in the bodies of His most consecrated followers His own marks.

There must have been much that was precious in these two clusters, which he and his Church needed to have pressed out, for them thus to have been bruised in the winepress. There must have been much choice metal in characters the Great Refiner took such trouble to purify. And have not the waxing and waning years proved this to be so? Few men or women born have done more to glorify God, and to bless His Church by lip, and life, and pen, than C. H. Spurgeon; while his dear and honoured wife has brought the divinest sunshine into the hearts and homes of many thousands of Christ's poor but consecrated servants. Neither the husband nor the wife have yet been estimated at their true worth. I know their only concern ever was to be acceptable unto *Him*; but it should be the care of Christ's own people to greatly honour those who have been greatly honoured by Him, and to esteem them highly in love for their work's sake.

The word *beautiful* used above for the life at Westwood was not descriptive only of the character and relationship of Mr. and Mrs. Spurgeon, but of the home itself. The taste displayed in all interior arrangements would have satisfied the most asthetic; while the gardens, grounds, and conservatories were ever a charm to the observer's eye and, when the master was with him to point out this beautiful feature and the other, a delight to his mind.

I ever admired, too, the wise consideration shown towards the servants. Their physical and spiritual welfare was as well cared for as any parents could reasonably desire for their daughters. I only wish some masters and mistresses 'who profess and call themselves Christians' would exemplify a little more of the spirit of our holy religion in this matter, remembering that 'they also have a Master in heaven.'

Mr. Spurgeon found in his garden a source of unceasing delight. I think he knew every single plant and flower his conservatories contained. He used to linger over them individually, as over verses in a chapter of the Bible when commenting thereon. 'There,' he would say, 'is not that exquisite? Look at the veins and colours in these leaves; don't you think God has put His own thoughts into them? This plant, for instance, has His laughable thoughts, this His loving thoughts, and this His serious ones; all Nature is full of God. His autograph is on every leaf and in every flower. All His creation speaks of Him and for Him.' We went into the vinery one day when the tree was in full leaf. He said, sniffing the odour from the branches, 'Well done, Solomon, the vines do give a *good* smell. You sniff, Williams - there is no fragrance, no perfume, nothing will describe it but *good*. You instinctively feel that it is healthy to take in the scent of a vine. I constantly meet with facts in Nature which go to confirm my belief in the verbal inspiration of Scripture.'

'Have you read Sir William Harcourt's speech, sir?' I asked him one day when we were sitting together in the arbour. 'No, not yet, but I want to. What does he say?' he replied. 'He says the Unionists are Troglodytes. What does he mean?' The word 'Troglodytes' was new to me; but I had looked up its meaning, and asked the question to see if he knew. He laughed and said, 'Oh, clever, is it not? Troglodytes, dwellers in caves, where they became blind.' Just then his man George brought to him the card of a gentleman who had called to see him.

'Ask him down, George.' The moment the visitor reached the arbour he said: 'Oh, Mr. Spurgeon, I only came to ask you not to trouble too much about these "Down-Graders." Remember what Elijah said, "I, even I, only am left;" yet God said, "Yet I have left me seven thousand in Israel, all the knees which have not bowed unto Baal, and every mouth which hath not kissed him."' 'Oh yes,' said Mr. Spurgeon, 'I always forgive old Elijah for having said that; and I don't think much of those other fellows, they were all Troglodytes. Why didn't they come out and help him?' The gentleman laughed, said little more, and departed.

John Ruskin, when he lived at Dulwich, attended the Tabernacle.

Mr. Spurgeon was not the man to be in the least affected by the presence of either men of letters, philosophers, statesmen, noblemen, or even kings and queens, and in turn he had them all to hear him. John Ruskin was a devoted attendant upon his ministry for years, and occasionally visited Mr. Spurgeon at his house. The pastor, when going over his valuable and extensive library of scientific, historical, and poetical books, which adorn the shelves of his beautiful drawing-room, pointed out to me a first edition of Ruskin's works, worth, he said, about 30*l.*, and which he had received as a gift from the author.[1] The two men, however, as the reader may easily imagine, were far from being in agreement upon many matters. Upon one occasion Mr. Ruskin told him he was fitted for something far better than constantly preaching to 'that herd at Newington.' This roused the preacher's righteous desire, and he gave the art-critic a pot of boiling oil on his head such as he would not be likely to forget for many a day.

When making another visit Mr. Ruskin said: 'Mr. Spurgeon, Paul was no gentleman.' 'Oh!' said the pastor, 'why so?' 'Well, he calls the man who differs from him a fool. He says: "Thou fool, that which thou sowest is not quickened except it die." Now, as a matter of fact, Paul was the fool, for he was ignorant of the process of the reproduction of the grain. That which is sown does not die; if it did it would abide alone.' 'Excuse me, Mr. Ruskin,' said Mr. Spurgeon, 'it is you who are ignorant, and not Paul, for you don't know what the true definition of death is; let me tell you. Death is the resolution of any compound body into its original elements. A grain of wheat is compound; when it is put into the ground it is actually resolved by the chemical action of the soil into its original clements, and that is its death; and out of the central germ of life is then produced the blade, the ear, and full corn in the ear; and if it did not so die it would

---

[1] He must have read them too. In one volume of his I have noticed half a dozen apt quotations from Ruskin.

abide alone. The apostle is right after all' Mr. Ruskin had to own himself defeated.

Many great and good men I met at Westwood. Dignitaries of the Church of England, noblemen, the foremost ministers of nearly every section of the Christian Church, and not a few of the leading laymen of the day, would now and again be found enjoying an hour with the man whom they all loved and honoured. 'I cannot tell, Williams,' he once said to me, 'how it is these Church of England men are so attached to me. I have said some very severe things about their Church, and yet I have many devoted friends among them. The Archbishop has told me to drive through his park whenever I like; and also to call upon him whenever I desire. I think it is because they admire honest outspokenness, even though it be against themselves.'

'I was having an argument with a clergyman one day,' Mr. Spurgeon once told me, 'who insisted that only ordained priests of the Church of England are in the true apostolic succession. "Well, what am I?" I said; "what do you fellows make of me? You cannot surely deny that God has set His seal upon my ministry!" "Oh, you are quite an exception," said the cleric; "I look upon you as a kind of Melchisedec. You had no predecessor, and you will have no successor. God has a right to make an exception if He so please." "If I am a Melchisedec, why don't you men pay me tithes, then?" I replied. He only answered with a smile; but he subsequently sent me a leg of pork; perhaps he considered it a tenth part of a pig he had killed.'

We were waiting at the gate at Westwood one Saturday afternoon for a Canon of the Church of England who had been invited to come and spend an hour with him. 'Which way will the Canon come, sir?' I asked. 'Oh, he will shoot in somehow,' he said. And shortly afterwards the worthy Canon did arrive, carrying in his hand a bag heavily laden with precious stones. He had obtained them to show Mrs. and Mr. Spurgeon. I have no idea to whom they belonged; nor can I now remember all their names. They enchanted us with their brilliance and beauty. There was one rare opal in which seemed mingled all the radiant colours of the rainbow; and a large ruby, to look into which the pastor said was 'like looking into a blast furnace.' Diamond, agate, amethyst, carbuncle, topaz, each and all of them excited both wonder and delight. As may well be supposed, the gratitude expressed to the Canon for the unexpected pleasure his visit had afforded was both abundant and intense. One of the things about Mr. Spurgeon's ministry, which often created astonishment in my own mind and in that of many others, was the masterly way in which he could bring all his knowledge to contribute parable, or point, or illustration, to his public utterances. Not many men could have used precious stones to so brighten and beautify a discourse as he once did when he said: 'As living stones in God's temple let your characters adorn it; as pearls exhibit the mild radiance of peace; as rubies, the ruddy hue of ardour; as sapphires, the bright light of joy; as emeralds, the restfulness of confidence; as diamonds, the transparency of a pure life.'

Lord Shaftesbury was, I think, one of the most interesting of all Mr. Spurgeon's friends whom I met at his house. To hear him talk about the Houses of Parliament, about the characters, opinions, and work of many members of both, was peculiarly interesting. With what pleasure would he dilate, too, upon the work being done on behalf of 'costers,' ragged-school children, and oppressed *employés* in many branches of work. Often some volume recently published would be the theme of conversation, which his lordship would analyse, criticise, approve, or condemn. Or he would give his opinion on many matters bearing on the welfare of our own and other nations; and especially on the prospects and general outlook of the Church and Kingdom of Christ. His mind was richly stored with Bible truths also, and I fancy he must have suggested not a few interesting subjects for sermons to the great preacher. His fund of rare and racy anecdotes was scarcely less exhaustible than that of Mr. Spurgeon, and many singular stories he used to tell of his own experience. He was fond of a bit of fun too. The story, I believe, is public property that after he had done so much for the costers and their donkeys, one said to him: 'I shall never look on a donkey again without thinking of your lordship;' but I fancy the following is known to but a few. He told Mr. Spurgeon that his housemaid had given notice to leave. He could not understand why. When, however, she was pressed for a reason, she said she did not like being personally alluded to at family prayer. His lordship was more bewildered than before. He had never made any personal reference to the housemaid that he knew of; but, as he read the prayers, he thought he would look over them. A possible explanation suggested itself which proved to be the solution of the matter. He found he had prayed 'for all things *that Thou hast made*,' and the young woman thought he said '*The Housemaid.*' Mr. Spurgeon told the story of a certain church-goer asking his vicar why he did not pray for the Prince of Wales. 'I do,' said the vicar. 'No,' said the man, 'you leave him out, for you pray for "All but Edward Prince of Wales."' The pastor had many funny illustrations to give us of the ridiculous effect of bad pronunciation on the part of preachers.

    That Lord Shaftesbury greatly esteemed Mr. Spurgeon and his work is evident from records he made in his diary. In 1875 he wrote: 'At eleven o'clock yesterday to Spurgeon's Tabernacle, to go with him over all his various institutions, school, college, almshouse, orphanage. All sound, good, true, Christian like. He is a wonderful man, full of zeal, affection, faith, abounding in reputation and authority, and yet perfectly humble, with the openness and simplicity of a child.' In 1881 he recorded a visit to Westwood: 'Drove to Norwood to see my friend Spurgeon. He is well, thank God, and admirably lodged. His place is lovely. His wife's health, too, is improved by change of residence. Pleasant and encouraging to visit such men and find them still full of perseverance, faith, joy, in the service of our blessed Lord.' In a letter written to Mr. Spurgeon he says: 'You must not admit any abatement of your regard and love for me. Mine towards you can never be lessened while you stand up so vigorously, so devotedly, so exclusively for our blessed Lord.'

Upon the occasion of Mr. Spurgeon's jubilee, Lord Shaftesbury took the chair, and in his diary wrote of the meeting: 'Yesterday to Metropolitan Tabernacle to preside over grand meeting in honour of Spurgeon's fiftieth birthday. A wonderful sight; nearly, if not quite, seven thousand adults, enthusiastic souls, crammed even to suffocation, by way of audience. Felt at first quite appalled. Had to make opening speech. Here, again, a *non nobis* must be "said or sung." By the blessing of our Lord, I was, as everyone said, equal to the occasion.'

I was present at this marvellous meeting as one of the speakers. Lord Shaftesbury says there were nearly, if not quite,. seven thousand present. But one of the deacons who looked after the building, and who ever spoke of the Tabernacle in the feminine gender, said to me: 'We counted eight thousand out of her; I don't know where she put 'em, but we did.' I sat between Mr. Spurgeon and Dr. Parker. The Doctor did not speak until near the end of the meeting. Mr. Spurgeon whispered to him, 'Doctor, I am keeping the big strawberry for the top of the basket.' 'All right,' said the Doctor.

When he did speak the enthusiasm of the meeting reached its culmination. The wit, sarcasm, eloquence, and happy citation of several texts of Scripture are not likely to be forgotten by those who were present. Mr. Spurgeon said when he had finished: 'Dr. Parker is himself, and he has spoken to us in such a way as we shall never forget.' The tribute paid by Lord Shaftesbury upon this occasion to Mr. Spurgeon's genius and goodness was worthy both of the man who gave it and of him to whom it was given.

Dr. Wayland, from America, came to see Mr. Spurgeon one Saturday. The Doctor was thus greeted: 'Hullo! Dr. Wayland, glad to see you. Are you the author of Wayland's *Moral Science*?' 'No,' replied the Doctor, 'the author of Wayland's *Moral Science* was the author of me.' The two men bubbled over with fun, and soon found each other's company specially congenial. Dr. Wayland was afterwards introduced to the students, and also to the ministers assembled for the annual conference, and not a few of them will retain pleasant and profitable recollections of the bright, witty, and stirring addresses of the worthy American.

Old George, Mr. Spurgeon's tried and trusted servant, was not only a great comfort to his master during his seasons of severe illness, but was ever and anon the occasion of pleasant and innocent merriment. He seemed to have learned the art of his master in making visitors to the house agreeable and pleasant. 'Old George does make me laugh,' the master said one day, 'and whenever I get low he is always trying to cheer me up. He said to me the other day: "Master, do you believe in ghosts? 'cause I don't, and I will tell you why. Don't you see, if a man goes to the good place he wonner want to come wandering about these regions any more. And if he goes to the bad place they wonner let him out even at the back door to get a drink of water. That's why I don't believe in ghosts."' As George came into the study one day Mr. Spurgeon said: 'Now Mr. Williams, here is a riddle for you. Why has George got white whiskers and black hair?' 'Give it up, sir.' 'Why, because he has used his jaws a lot more than his brains!'

All the world knows that Mr. Spurgeon now and again enjoyed a cigar. I have seen not a few caricatures representing him smoking a pipe, but he never used a pipe all the years I knew him. But a cigar he certainly did, now and again, really enjoy. Dr. --, of America, when requested to give a short address after the sermon at the Tabernacle one Sunday evening, spoke of his having given up the sin of smoking. Mr. Spurgeon's reply is memorable. He had often found a weary brain soothed by a cigar. He did not consider he did wrong in smoking. He had been speaking that night about real sins, not imaginary ones. He found enough to do to keep ten Commandments, and until he found the eleventh, 'Thou shalt not smoke,' he should enjoy a cigar to the glory of God. This, and the controversy it excited in many newspapers, is familiar to the minds of many.

The following will indicate how absolutely Mr. Spurgeon had his habit of smoking under control. 'Enjoying your bacca again, sir,' said old George one day when his master was lighting a cigar. 'I can do without my bacca a good deal easier than you can, George,' said the master. 'I don't believe you can, sir.' 'Very well, George, don't you smoke again until I do.' 'Agreed, sir.' A week passed, a fortnight. Poor old George was dying for his pipe. One was asked to intercede with the master that George might be allowed to have a pipe. 'No, no!' said Mr. Spurgeon. 'He made a bargain, and let him stick to it.' Eventually George was allowed to smoke, but Mr. Spurgeon did not have a cigar for months after that.

Some twenty-five to thirty years ago, an excursion had been

organised by one of the young men's classes at the Tabernacle to Mid-Surrey, and as Mr. Spurgeon lived at Nightingale Lane, Clapham, a call was to be made with the brake to pick him up on the road. It was a beautiful early morning, and on arriving all were in high spirits, pipes and cigars alight, and looking forward to a day of unrestrained enjoyment. He was ready waiting at the gate, jumped up to the box-seat reserved for him, and, looking round with astonishment, exclaimed, 'What, gentlemen! are you not ashamed to be smoking so early?' Here was a damper! Dismay was on every face. Pipes and cigars one by one failed and dropped out of sight. When all had disappeared, out came his cigar-case; he lit up and smoked away serenely. Astonishment was now on every face. One of the party nearest to him said, 'I thought you said you objected to smoking, Mr. Spurgeon?' 'Oh no,' he replied; 'I did not say I objected. I asked if they were not ashamed, and it appears they were, for they have put them all out.' And he puffed away quite serenely.

Many were the funny things he said to me about cigars, but I will leave them among the thousand and one innocent pleasantries which, however enjoyed when uttered, will be better preserved in my memory than in these recorded reminiscences. But just one choice bit of pleasant shrewdness I must mention. Some gentleman wrote to Mr. Spurgeon saying 'he had heard he smoked, and could not believe it true. Would Mr. Spurgeon write and tell him if it really was so?' The reply sent was as follows:

DEAR --, - I cultivate my flowers and burn my weeds.
Yours truly,
C. H. SPURGEON

Upon his return from Mentone he used to relate to me with great delight many of the experiences of his holiday season. The following, however, was told me by a friend, although Mr. Spurgeon himself alluded to it. He came in contact during one of his visits to the South with an eminent medical man also staying there. At the time the doctor did not know who Mr. Spurgeon was. The subject of certain ailments and diseases came up in the course of conversation. Mr. Spurgeon went so fully into the questions under discussion, and gave such accurate diagnoses of a number of maladies flesh is heir to, and of the treatment which, in his judgment, was best suited to them; and manifested also such an intimate scientific knowledge with the organism of the human body, that the doctor looked at him with blank astonishment. He afterwards inquired who he was, saying, 'He is the most remarkable man I ever met. He seems to me to know as much about the human body and almost every form of disease as any medical man I know. He would have made a splendid physician.'

One day, during the winter of 1888, a celebrated portrait painter called upon him with a friend, who knew Mr. Spurgeon, at the Hôtel Beau-Rivage, to ask him to sit for his portrait. The artist was very pressing in his request to be favoured with a sitting, to which Mr. Spurgeon smilingly replied: 'You cannot paint me, Mr. --. You know Mr. -- [mentioning another well-known portrait painter]; I sat several times at his urgent request. On the fourth or fifth occasion he threw down his brush with the remark, "I cannot paint your portrait, Mr. Spurgeon. You have sat to me four or five times, and you have never looked twice alike. Your face seems quite altered on each occasion."' Needless to say this remark put the closure upon the request, for the artist replied, 'Well, if he could not paint your portrait, I am sure I cannot.'

At another time, referring to a photograph some one had sent for his approval for publication, he remarked: 'Yes, very good; as good as can be of a man as ugly as myself. I have heard there has been only one well known person not as good-looking as I am, and that was King --,' mentioning one of the crowned heads of Europe.

There never was a man who cared less for personal appearance than Mr. Spurgeon. He once said: 'The best way to dress is as Hannah More did, so neatly that nobody shall ever notice how you are dressed.' He was always singularly neat and orderly in his attire, but nothing more. Fashion to him was folly, and as for special *ministerial* attire, he cared nothing. The 'wide-awake' hat, inseparable from him, was an indication of the ease of his mind as to 'wherewithal shall we be clothed.' Of personal vanity he had absolutely none. Many a bit of fun I have heard him poke at ministers from his own college who had gone in for clerical-cut coat and stiff all-round collar, but always with the utmost good-humour and kindliness of spirit. About the 'wide-awake' hat he has said many odd things. He supposed they were called wide-awake because there was no nap on them. When they came out they were a *felt* necessity. It was very incongruous for a minister to have a wide-awake hat and a *sleepy* heart.

'I was driving a week or two ago at Mentone,' he said once, 'when the coachman thought he had got a rare sight for us. Pointing his whip upwards to a flock of birds, he cried out excitedly, *"Eagles! eagles! eagles!"* But the poor chap seemed very disappointed when I said, "No, no, man! not eagles. The eagle is an imperial bird; it never goes in flocks, but always alone; those are only kites."'

Saturdays at Westwood gave me an education in the matter of many choice books, and I seldom came away without one or two. But it was a greater treat still to hear Mr. Spurgeon read some charming poem or instructive chapter himself. I remember, when

Miss Havergal's poems, *Under the Surface,* were issued, how he revelled in them. The one entitled 'From Glory unto Glory' he read one evening 'over the tea-cups.' His eyes sparkled with delight and filled with tears of joy, as he reached the third and fourth stanzas of that magnificent song -

> From glory unto glory! our faith hath seen the King,
> We own His matchless beauty, as adoringly we sing;
> But He hath more to show us! O thought of untold bliss!
> And we press on exultingly in certain hope to this.
>
> To marvellous outpourings of His 'treasures new and old,'
> To largeness of His bounty, paid in the King's own gold,
> To glorious expansion of His mysteries of grace,
> To radiant unveilings of the brightness of His face.

Speaking of the gifted authoress of these poems, he said to me afterwards: 'There is a centre to every storm where perfect calm reigns. There is a point within the circle of the most consuming flame where life is possible without any danger of its being consumed. Miss Havergal seems to me to have got into the very centre of the storms that are disturbing others, and abides in perfect peace. She seems to have penetrated to the very heart of God who is a consuming fire, and rests absolutely in His love. She never could have written as she has except for an extraordinary intimacy with God.'

We had several talks on different occasions about Shakespeare. He had read all his plays, and some of them many times. He greatly admired the advice given by Polonius to his son:

Give thy thoughts no tongue
Nor any unproportioned thought his act,
Be thou familiar, but by no means vulgar, etc.

He gave me an incident from his own experience of how some men made true friendship with them impossible, because they all owed a slight familiarity such license as to border on vulgarity. 'There was Mr. --. You knew him, did you not? He was a big man in his way, and seemed very anxious to count me as his friend. He was very hospitable and generous. I was friendly and agreeable with him. Then he began to call me "Charles." I looked at him. I did not mind it much, but had he been my father or brother he could scarcely have done more. I thought I would let him see how it looked, so I called him *"John."* He did not see my purpose, and so went on to call me *"Charley."* Then I called him *"Jack;"* that cured him, and he dropped it. But I could see he had little of the sense of propriety.'

'We had a rare meeting at the Tabernacle the other night,' he said one day. 'Mr. -- spoke. My word! he has some force and power in him. He blundered in his grammar fearfully, his tropes and figures were terribly mixed, but all his mistakes were only like the rust on a cannon ball. He hit just as straight and hard as if he had not had them. I don't think any good could come of telling a man like him what mistakes he makes. It would probably rob him of much of his power if he knew it.'

Any who were much in Mr. Spurgeon's company, or who have read to any extent his sermons, must have soon been impressed with his intense and intelligent love of Nature. In one of his sermons he speaks strongly against the spirituality which leads men to shut their eyes to the beauties in the natural world. He says: 'I remember sorrowfully reading the expressions of a godly person, who in sailing down one of the most famous rivers in the world closed his eyes, lest the picturesque beauties of the scene should divert his mind from Scriptural topics. This may be regarded by some as profound spirituality; to me it savours of absurdity. There may be persons who think they have grown in grace when they have attained to this; it seems to me they are growing out of their senses. To despise the creating works of God, what is it but, in a measure, to despise God Himself? Milton's *Paradise Regained* is certainly inferior to his *Paradise Lost*, but the Eternal God has no inferior productions. All His works are masterpieces. There is no quarrel between Nature and Revelation, only fools think so; to wise men the one illustrates and establishes the other … Whoever may neglect the volume of Creation or the volume of Revelation, I shall delight in them both as long as I live.' I had many proofs that he did delight in both. But I shall never forget the joy he manifested one Saturday over a volume published by the Religious Tract Society on *Apples and Oranges: Talks with Children on Fruits*. He revelled in its pages with the simplicity and delight of a child. He said it had opened up to him a new world of wonders. Then he brought out a volume by the same authoress, Mrs. Dyson, on *Children's Flowers*, also published by the Religious Tract Society, and in which he found equal delight. In reviewing the latter in the *Sword and Trowel*, I do not wonder he wrote: 'Beautiful! beautiful! Please, papa, buy Maggie a copy, and mamma and yourself will like to read it. A half-crown cannot be better spent at the bookseller's; we are delighted with the little book. We never knew so much before about buttercups and daisies, dandelions and primroses. We have had the utmost pleasure in the perusal of this most interesting work.'

One of the most helpful experiences I had at Westwood was in connection with the family prayer. At six o'clock all the household gathered into the study for worship. I was sometimes asked to pray, but usually, and happily, Mr. Spurgeon would take the exercises of reading and praying himself. The portion read was invariably accompanied with exposition. How amazingly helpful those homely and gracious comments were! I remember, above many, his reading in Luke xxiv.: 'Jesus Himself drew near and went with them.' How sweetly he talked upon having Jesus with us wherever we go! Not only to have Him draw near at special seasons, but to draw near and go with us to whatever labour we undertake. Oh, the nearness of communion possible between Jesus and His own! It was *Jesus Himself* who drew near. It is well to have the joy of Christian fellowship, well to have the servants of Christ near us, or to have His Word near us; but to have Jesus Himself, the Lord of earth and heaven, to draw near and go with us, what a dignified privilege! What a delightful experience! This is indeed heaven below. 'O fools, and slow of heart to believe.' It is well to have Jesus with us, though He should call us fools. He shows us our folly only to make us wise. Our folly is never greater than when we do not believe, for unbelief is the very essence of folly; and so on.

How full, too, of tender pleading, of serene confidence in God, of world-embracing sympathy, were Mr. Spurgeon's prayers! With what gracious familiarity he could talk with his Divine Master! Yet what reverence ever marked his address to his Lord! His public prayers were an inspiration and benediction, but his prayers in the family were to me more wonderful still. The *beauty* of them was ever striking; figures, symbols, citations of choice Scriptural emblems, all given with a spontaneity and naturalness that charmed the mind and moved the heart, and served to bring home the conviction that Mr. Spurgeon bowed before God in family prayer appeared a grander man even than when holding thousands spellbound by his oratory. I would rather pray like Mr. Spurgeon than preach like an archangel. The thoughtfulness and deep solicitude for the welfare of all 'the servants of our King' was also a gracious feature of his intercessions. He would make reference to any special circumstances or needs represented by those kneeling with him; but all Christians, in all conditions and in all spheres of service, were remembered by him. Often have I risen from my knees strengthened as Daniel was when the mysterious hand had laid its gentle pressure upon his head. I owe much, my people owe much, to the family prayers at Westwood.

Then the good man would give himself up to the preparation of his Sunday sermons. Sometimes he would ask me to wait a little while alone with him, and we would talk some subjects over; then he would say, 'You had better go now, my sermon pangs have come.' And there alone with God and His Word were born those mighty 'messages to the multitudes' which have blessed hundreds of thousands in this generation, and which will continue increasingly to bless millions all the world over until our Lord shall come. The work done by C. H. Spurgeon cannot die. 'I beseech you,' I once heard him say, 'to live not only for this age, but for the next also. I would fling my shadow through eternal ages if I could.' He has done it. His work is as imperishable as the truth of God. His memory shall not fade like a vanishing star, nor his works be forgotten like a dying echo. He will shine on, never ceasing to brighten human lives by the truth he preached, the work he accomplished, and the stainless life he lived.

CHAPTER IV

RURAL RAMBLES

MR. SPURGEON was a prodigious worker. Although a man of great physical stamina, the amount accomplished astonished all who knew him. The effort of preaching on each Lord's Day to the immense multitudes which gathered to hear him would have been enough to break down any ordinary constitution. Ministers who have taken a service now and again at the Tabernacle have often expressed their surprise that the pastor could stand the strain, year after year, as he did. Then there was the second service, the Communion, each Lord's Day, generally held in the Lecture Hall, but once a month in the Tabernacle itself. Into the conduct of these Communion Services he would put his whole soul, not infrequently giving at them the most choice addresses that ever came from his lips. In addition to this, he was frequently occupied for nearly an hour seeing visitors from all parts of the world who had come to hear him and were anxious to shake his hand. On each Monday morning the weekly sermon was ready for revision. This entailed close application for several hours; while for many years Monday afternoons were spent with the students in the college. Later there were officers' meetings or great tea meetings to attend, or inquirers to see; and from seven o'clock until eight thirty the large prayer meeting in the Tabernacle, at which he gave addresses often equal in length to ordinary sermons. He was frequently at the Tabernacle on Tuesday, sometimes for many hours, and when not there he was, in all probability, preaching away from home, or speaking at some great meeting. Thursday night he preached again, when many of his most helpful sermons were delivered. Friday he was ever found, except when ill, giving his weekly lecture to the students; and often staying to attend to other business up to seven or eight o'clock, and occasionally even to a late hour, on account of some special meeting. When one thinks, in addition to all this toil, of the labours entailed in editing the *Sword and Trowel*, the frequent issue of books, the writing of innumerable letters, and the thousand and one matters connected with his own institutions, and the cares of many Churches demanding his attention, one cannot but wonder how it was all accomplished.

In two matters lay the secret - he had vast capacity for work, and he redeemed with great jealousy every hour of his time. He frequently told us as students to be sure and read John Foster's essay on 'The Improvement of Time.' He had evidently done so himself, and ever sought to act up to its teaching. He was not an advocate for working very early in the morning, as some have been. When speaking of Barnes's *Notes* once he said: 'Barnes used to rise at four o'clock each morning, and he is said to have written these notes before breakfast; perhaps if he had slept a little longer and written them after breakfast they would have been better worth reading.' Yet not infrequently did he do a large share of work in summer time from break of day. He wrote me once to take the 10.25 train from London Bridge for Dorking, and he would meet me at Sutton Junction. When he got into the railway carriage he said: 'Well, friend

Williams, did you do any work before you came away?' 'Yes, sir. I was in my study from half-past six until nine o'clock,' I replied. 'Oh,' he said, 'I was in my study at half-past four. I had five hours of solid work before I left, so I think I may enjoy my holiday.' He frequently warned us in the college against working 'far into the night,' as many students have done. He said: 'Gentlemen, if you want to *shorten your days*, lengthen your nights.' He alluded to one eminent preacher and lecturer who sat frequently far into the night, with wet cloths wrapped about his head, polishing his sentences, rounding his periods, and making yet more perfect his perorations. 'Do you think God ever intended His servants to do that?' he said.

Mr. Spurgeon's *laborious* life made frequent relaxations an imperative necessity. He found not a little 'unbending of the bow' in changing the subjects of his study; in the reading of historical, scientific, and poetical works; with occasional dips into books of fun and humour. An hour or two in his grounds would at times afford all the relaxation his work would allow. Years ago I now and again played a game of bowls with him. I remember him saying, 'This is the game the old Puritans liked. It was from it they got the term "bias of the will," and a bias it has, and no mistake.' I did not see him play many games in later years. For exercise he at one time tried horse-riding. 'But I did not cut a good figure on horseback,' he said; 'and once I was told by a passer-by that I had better get inside, I should be safer there.'

In an essay on the Sabbath, published some time ago, the opinion is expressed that ministers whose calling demands the fullest exercise of their powers on each Lord's Day should be careful not to miss the blessing originally designed by the institution of the Sabbath, and that there would be less mortality amongst Christian ministers if the law of one day's rest in seven had been less violated.

The essay goes on to say: 'While only doing the Lord's work on the Lord's Day, would it not be also showing a deeper regard for the Sabbath, ordained for our physical and mental well being, if we sought on another day to observe the letter and spirit of this institution?' These sentiments Mr. Spurgeon endorsed, both for *himself and his horses.* As he drove to the Tabernacle he called his horses Jews and Saturday he made their Sabbath. For himself, when possible, Wednesday was his day of weekly rest. I do not say he always abstained from mental toil on this day, but that when he could he sought on this middle day of the week that relaxation from his exacting labours so essential in every case to the maintenance of mental vigour and elasticity of soul. His weekly rest has turned many a Wednesday to me into a day

> Most calm, most bright,
> The fruit of this, the next world's bud,
> The indorsement of supreme delight.
>
> The couch of time, care's balm and bay.

At Essex, the county of his birth, Mr. Spurgeon poked many a bit of innocent fun. 'Essex is the Galilee of England, and Coggeshall the Nazareth of Essex.' 'Essex is one of our eastern counties. Wise men come from the East, and show their wisdom in coming from it.' This, of course, is only pleasantry, for he ever loved the scenes of his childhood, and found his last visit, made a few months before his fatal illness, to be full of inspiration and happy memories, for he speaks of having enjoyed himself mightily. But Surrey, the county of his adoption, was ever 'the garden of England' to him.

Years ago he wrote: 'England for me for a country, Surrey for a county, and for a village give me - no, I shan't tell you, or you will be hunting John Ploughman up.' In the same chapter he says: 'There is a glorious view from the top of Leith Hill, in our dear old Surrey; and Hindhead, and Martha's Chapel, and Boxhill are not to be sneezed at.' Those acquainted with 'dear old Surrey' will not wonder that he should be so delighted with it. Its scenery is as full of charm and pleasant variety as that of any county in Britain. Its smiling hills and richly wooded valleys, its streams, rivulets, and rivers, its lovely nooks and quiet corners, its fertile fields, its tiny villages, its country mansions and churches with interesting historical associations, all go to make it one of the prettiest and most interesting counties of England. To the geologist, botanist, historian, and antiquarian, few counties could afford richer instruction; while to those seeking refreshment for tired brain and weary heart its ever-diversified scenery of homely hamlets, verdant valleys, picturesque uplands, romantic heights, naked heaths, shady dells, and plains covered with a carpet of living green, will minister health and vigour as few other scenes can.

Mr. Spurgeon seemed familiar with every sequestered nook and quiet sylvan road for many miles from his own house. He must have studied, too, the histories of many of its churches, mansions, and quiet little towns; while of its three rivers - the Wey, the Wandle, and the Mole - he had ever some fresh and interesting remark to make. We were sitting one lovely summer's day on the banks of the Wandle, at Carshalton, the place celebrated by Fuller for its 'trout and walnuts.' The river was low, and we watched with interest the springs bubbling up in the river bed and flowing into the expanse of water formed in the centre of the village. He traced for my benefit the course of the stream from Croydon, where it rises, westward by Waddon and Beddington, through Carshalton, then northward by

Mitcham, and Merton, and Wandsworth, to the Thames - a distance in all of about eleven miles. Of the Wandle and its neighbourhood Ruskin thus writes in his *Crown of Wild Olives*:

'Twenty years ago, there was no lovelier piece of lowland scenery in South England, nor any more pathetic in the world, by its expression of sweet human character and life, than that immediately bordering on the sources of the Wandle, and including the low moors of Addington, and the villages of Beddington and Carshalton, with all their pools and streams. No clearer or diviner waters ever sang with sweet constant lips of the hand which "giveth rain from heaven"; no pastures ever lightened in springtime with more passionate blossoming; no sweeter homes ever hallowed the heart of the passer-by with their pride of peaceful gladness - fair-hidden - yet full-confessed … The welling of stainless waters, trembling and pure, like a body of light, enters the pool of Carshalton, cutting itself a radiant channel down to the gravel, through warp of feathery weeds, all waving, which it traverses with its deep thread of clearness, like the chalcedony in moss-agate, starred here and there with the white grenouillette.' He deplores 'the slow stealing of aspects of reckless, indolent, animal neglect, over the delicate sweetness of that English scene'; but still much of the original beauty abides.

The Wey did not so often cross our path, its course being from the borders of Hampshire, where it rises, along the south-western side of Surrey, on to Guildford, Weybridge, and the Thames, and thus remote from the scenes of our rural rambles. But he was as well acquainted with its line of flow as with the Wandle itself, and seemed interested to trace to their sources even its tributary streams, which descend from the Devil's Punchbowl, Leith Hill, Thursley and Witley, Pirbright and Chobham Common. The waters of the Wey were spoken of as much less fertilising than those of the Mole. Pope, in *Windsor Forest*, speaks of

> The chalky Wey, that rolls a milky wave.

But its wave is often far from 'milky,' and especially after heavy showers, for these wash large quantities of sand into the river from the steep hills near Godalming, and make its waters turbid.

The Mole was, however, his favourite river.

> Here traceable, there hidden; there again
> To sight restored, and glittering in the sun.

'Here is the Mole again, Williams,' he would say as we drove over or alongside its gentle current. The course of this river is much longer than that of the Wandle, but he seemed to know every mile of verdant country through which it flowed. Its origin is in some bubbling springs on elevated ground on the northern borders of Sussex, near the two Horsham lines of the London and Brighton Railway. Then it meanders on to Betchworth, around the base of Boxhill, through the richly wooded vale of Mickleham to Leatherhead, then through the meadows at Cobham, to Esher Place, East Moulsey, and joins 'the silver-breasted Thames' opposite Hampton Court. Perhaps one reason why the Mole had special attraction for him was the fact of it having found a place in the flowery numbers and classic pages of not a few of our eminent British poets; for he knew this, and would speak of the references made to it by Pope in his *Windsor Forest*, Thomson in his Seasons, Spenser in his *Marriage of the Thames and Medway*. Milton speaks of

The sullen Mole that runneth underneath.

Spenser's reference is

And Mole, that like a nousling mole, doth make
His way still under ground, till Thames he o'ertake.

Thomson writes of

The soft windings of the silent Mole,

and Pope of

The sullen Mole that hides his diving flood.

While a minor poetess, Miss Bethune, describing its picturesque journey, says

......in its waveless course
The Mole glides on, through quiet meadows, rich
In yellow cowslips, and the tall foxglove,
With its deep purple bells, dew laden.

Many were the illustrations and figures of speech these rambles by the rivers suggested to Mr. Spurgeon. Often, when resting on a post or leaning against a gate, his talk would be of matters far removed from rural scenes and subjects. I remember such sentences as the following:

If Science were to make a creed she would commit suicide.

I regard the style of John Bunyan as being the nearest approach

THE MOLE

to the style of the Lord Jesus than that of any man who has ever written.

What a wonderful creation the human mind is! The other day I counted eight sets of thoughts which had been passing through my mind at once while I was preaching.

The deacons of -- came to me the other day requesting me to ask their minister to preach better. He is a man of ability and repute; but they say his sermons are very milk-and-watery. I am afraid it is so; but why could they not tell him themselves?

They have been asking lately, 'Is life worth living?' to which *Mr. Punch* has replied, 'That depends on the liver.' But to this he might have added, what many a clergyman would answer, 'That depends on the living.'

They say, 'A bird in the hand is worth two in the bush,' but I believe one bird in God's hand is worth fifty in my bush. What do you think of that for a proverb?

Was not that address by Mr. Birrell at Maze Pond the other day beautiful? 'John did no miracle; but all things John spake of this Man were true.' He has made this text more precious to me than it was before. I should like to earn the encomium, 'All that Spurgeon spake of this Man was true.' Any preacher of whom this can be said can be well content without doing miracles. I must preach from this testimony to John.

He did shortly afterwards give a very beautiful address from it to the students, and has since preached from it in the Tabernacle.

One of Mr. Spurgeon's sources of special enjoyment when out rural ising was in leaving his carriage and walking through village

BEDDINGTON VILLAGE

churches and churchyards. He would read the inscriptions and epitaphs on the tombstones, jot down texts inscribed on them, and sometimes pass very quaint remarks on what he read.

'You can always tell,' he once remarked, 'whether the rector of a church is Ritualistic or Evangelical, by the way the church and churchyard are kept. The Evangelicals are not nearly so careful to keep the places neat and tidy as the High Churchmen are. What a pity it is! Yet I fear me the very care taken of these material things savours of superstition. They have the idea that spiritual qualities can adhere to material substances, but they can't.'

On another occasion he referred to Disestablishment, and said: 'The clergy say if the Church of England is disestablished there will be no recognition of religion by our Houses of Parliament; and we shall be practically a heathen nation, so far as official recognition of religion is concerned. But it need not, indeed cannot, be so. That form of doctrine and worship observed by the majority of our countrymen should be the one represented in Parliament, and upon all public or state occasions when a religious service is desirable.'

We walked up to the *altar* in one church. 'Christ is the only altar we have or need,' said he. 'I wonder why, if they call them altars, they always put them against the wall; the altar under the Old Dispensation could not have been so placed, for the Psalmist says, "So will I *compass* Thine altar, O Lord!"'

Beddington Church afforded him many subjects of interesting study. Over its handsome monuments, curiously ornamented tombstones, quaint inscriptions, attractive memorial tablets, and illustrative windows, he used to linger in earnest thought and with no little pleasure; while meditations among the sepulchral memorials and many tombstones with quaint or suggestive epitaphs in the churchyard gave inspiration to not a few of his recorded proverbs and even published discourses.

It is commonly reported that many authors have found in their publishers a source of irritation and annoyance, and have secretly endorsed the well-known epigrammatic sentence, 'Now, Barabbas was a publisher.' Messrs. Passmore & Alabaster, Mr. Spurgeon's publishers, stood in the relationship to him of close and intimate friends. Mr. Passmore was a member of New Park Street when the young preacher from Waterbeach accepted the pastorate, and at once a friendship between them was formed which remained unbroken to the last. The friendship with Mr. Alabaster began at a later date, and although he was a staunch Churchman, it was equally close and real. I remember Mr. Passmore coming to Westwood one Saturday, when Mr. Spurgeon gave him a gentle reproof because he had not been to see him for a week or two. 'Why did you stay away?' said the pastor; to which his friend replied, 'Because of what Solomon says: "Withdraw thy foot from thy neighbour's house, lest he be weary of thee."' 'Well,' said Mr. Spurgeon playfully, 'that is perverting Scripture with a vengeance. How could I ever be weary of thee? You ought to know better than make such bad use of Solomon as that.' Then Mr. Passmore tried to induce him to alter the title of his volume of *Farm Sermons*; but the author was firm, and would not yield to any alternative one suggested. 'The title is short, sententious, and expresses admirably the nature of the book. I don't think we shall find a better.'

Many happy hours have I spent, together with Mr. Spurgeon, with these publishers, whose names, being ever on Mr. Spurgeon's works, are known throughout the civilised world. Exceedingly pleasant are the recollections I have of both. In addition to his having them to stay with him in turns at Mentone, Mr. Spurgeon would now and again have them for a day's outing in Surrey. I had the privilege on one occasion of making the fourth of the party. The day was beautifully fine, and Mr. Spurgeon was as happy 'as a lawyer in Term time or a physician in November ;' and he made us feel also, as Sylvester expresses it, 'as happy as Heaven's angels, or as birds in their bowers.' Mr. Passmore, though usually a quiet and self-possessed man, caught such a fit of laughing at some of the exceedingly funny stories the pastor told us, and at the unusually witty things he said, that at luncheon eating seemed almost out of the question. Mr. Spurgeon's face was a study indeed; I have seldom seen anything like the expression then on his countenance in any of his portraits. The artist at Mentone told him how it changed. He would have thought so if he had seen him then. The sanctified comicality his wondrous eyes and charming lineaments expressed, must remain a bright mental picture only to the three friends then in

BEDDINGTON CHURCH

council with him, or to perhaps a few others also who have looked into his expressive features when they beamed with the healing medicine of mirth, or were illumined with the sunshine of infinite love, and the ineffable commingling of the joy, human and divine, his heart possessed.

What made this day's outing one of peculiar pleasure to both author and publishers was, I think, the completion of the great work, *The Treasury of David*. But of this I cannot speak positively. I only remember that very little was said about either writing or publishing, but a great deal about the beauties of Nature and our Heavenly Father's wondrous love. It fell to my lot to give a stanza or two from Milton, and to undergo another examination as to my knowledge of the trees. Mr. Passmore ever and anon recalled some interesting event connected with the early days of Mr. Spurgeon's ministry, while Mr. Alabaster treated us to some bit of history associated with the neighbourhood through which we were passing.

We drove from Dorking along the upper road to Guildford, but turned out of our way for an hour or so to call at the historic mansion of Mr. Evelyn at Wotton. Mr. Evelyn, lately Member of Parliament for Deptford, was intimate with Mr. Spurgeon. He did not know his illustrious friend was calling, but, happily, we found Mr. Evelyn at home, and a very warm and hearty welcome we all received.

Wotton House has been the seat of the Evelyn family since the days of Queen Elizabeth. Here lived the famous author of the *Evelyn Diary*, which deals largely with domestic manners and morals of the later Stuart times. The situation of this famous house is thus described in the first volume of the *Diary*: 'The House large and ancient, suitable to those hospitable times, and so sweetly environed with those delicious streams and venerable woods, as in the judgement of Strangers as well as Englishmen, it may be compared to one of the most pleasant Seats in the Nation, and most tempting for a great person and wanton purse to render it conspicuous.' The situation, at the junction of two valleys, is in the midst of the most charming scenery; while the view from the magnificent Leith Hill hard by, the highest point in Surrey, is such as can scarcely be surpassed for picturesqueness anywhere in England.

Within the mansion itself there are many valuable heirlooms. Mr. Evelyn afforded us great pleasure by pointing out not a few of these rare objects of interest, almost priceless in value. The original manuscripts of the *Diary* were there: the Prayer-book from which the Burial Service was read at the execution of Charles I., with a stain of blood from the King's neck on its page (Mr. Spurgeon smiled at this, but Mr. Evelyn had no doubt about the matter); the famous picture of Sylva Evelyn, by Sir Godfrey Kneller, which has been engraved as a frontispiece to his *Diary*, as well as hundreds of other curios and treasures. We had no time to visit Wotton Church, although assured that monuments, memorials, and inscriptions of singular and unique interest were to be found there. With many thanks we bade the kind and genial owner of this charming and historic seat a hearty farewell.

Almost the last time Mr. Spurgeon and I drove together through Surrey I remember passing an 'old iron' yard, in which were standing two worn-out old traction engines. 'There, Williams,' said he, 'are two portraits of what we shall soon be - all the steam gone out of us, our faculties used up, the potent fires of our being spent.' 'Not yet, sir, I hope,' said I. 'Ah! you don't know how soon, dear fellow,' said he. Nothing was said for a minute, but a world of deep feeling was crowded into those few moments of silence. He was far from well then. Little did I think how soon the potent fires of one mighty engine would be put out - no, not put out, taken out, to burn yet more brightly in other service. On the last occasion I heard him preach he said: 'I shall not finish preaching when I have done with earth; I expect to preach to principalities, to constellations, in yon brighter world.' It may be he has done this ere now. Moments and space are annihilated where only eternity is in the calculation.

Mr. Alabaster and I had another delightful holiday with him at Eastbourne once. The Queen's Hotel was his favourite quarter when stopping at this bourne, from which he ever reluctantly returned. We had several delightful excursions in Sussex. One to Burling Gap proved specially interesting, for we witnessed a practice with life-saving apparatus by a number of Coastguardsmen. These exercises were not only pleasant to see, but they afforded also many suggestive illustrations for sermons. We visited Wilmington, where the giant is. It was said to be of Celtic origin, as the Romans never represented their figures as nude. To Lullington we went also, where the smallest Anglican Church in England is to be seen. It seats fifteen people; but when the bishop of the diocese preached there, twenty-six were said to be squeezed in. The size is thirteen feet by sixteen, and is said to be part of a larger church which once stood there. We drove to Litlington, where the delightful gardens are. The place takes its name from a meadow, and was probably originally 'Little Meadow Town.' It is a lovely spot. No wonder Eastbourne excursionists resort thither in such numbers!

Occasionally our ruralising was in Kent. Hayes, where the Hon. Thomas Walpole lived, and where the illustrious William Pitt was born, he never wearied of visiting; while on the common hard by many recreative hours were spent. On Keston Heath the

Ravensbourne rises, and then
>Wanders in Hayes and Bromley, Beckenam Vale,
>And struggling Lewisham, to where Deptford Bridge
>Uprises, in obedience to its flood.

At Lewisham it unites with the Lee, and at Deptford Creek joins the Thames. At Keston not a few bright seasons of rest were enjoyed, while all the roads and lanes for miles around became familiar sights by reason of frequent drives. Of Keston, here is what Mr. Spurgeon himself said:

It is generally admitted that the scenery around London, including portions of some half-dozen counties, is as fascinating to rambling lovers of Nature as very many of those landscapes which tourists travel hundreds of miles to see. The great city and its far-reaching suburbs, however, cover so vast an area that, hitherto, the inhabitants of one side of it have known little or nothing respecting the sunny landscapes and shady lanes on the other side twenty miles distant. People can now explore these fair regions, one at a time, on the Saturday half holiday which has been given them for the purpose. Many prefer to walk, for the hardy pedestrian enjoys advantages of observation above all other travellers. From one of those books which reveal the beauties of these environs, entitled *Round Bromley and Keston*, we borrow an illustration.

Keston itself is one of the most charming of villages, but our space will only allow of our noticing Holwood Park, the favourite residence of William Pitt at the end of the last century. 'When I was a boy I used to go bird nesting in the wood at Holwood,' once remarked the great statesman, 'and it was always my wish to call it my own.' That wish was duly gratified; and Pitt's friend, George Rose, says that 'he took the greatest delight in his residence at Holwood, which he enlarged and improved (it may be truly said) with his own hands. Often have I seen him working in his woods and gardens with his labourers for whole days together, undergoing considerable bodily fatigue, and with so much eagerness and assiduity that you would suppose the cultivation of his estate to be the principal occupation of his life.' Wilberforce was accustomed to visit his friend at Holwood, and to share in his favourite recreations. Thus one day, in April 1790, after breakfast, 'we sallied forth armed with bill-hooks,' writes the Abolitionist, 'cutting new walks from one large tree to another through the thickets of the Holwood copses.' Since those days the estate has been much altered, the houses have been rebuilt, and some of Pitt's plantations levelled; but still one rare relic remains in the old tree of our engraving, now called Emancipation Oak. In Wilberforce's diary for 1785 we read:

At length, I well remember, after a conversation with Mr. Pitt in the open air, at the root of an old tree at Holwood, just above the deep descent into the Vale of Keston, I resolved to give notice on a fit occasion in the House of Commons of my intention to bring forward the abolition of the slave trade.

The seat by the side of the tree was erected twenty years ago by Earl Stanhope, by permission of Lord Cranworth, who then owned the estate. A tree with such associations may claim near relationship with the most celebrated of its species, with that tribe of Gospel oaks which dot the surface of England. It was because he had the spirit of Christ in so eminent a degree that Wilberforce acted as he did; and no man other than a chosen vessel in God's hand would have been so successful in his lifework. Has not the great Captain of our salvation other men to whom He will commit other glorious works? Not yet are men delivered from the curse of strong drink, nor from the opium tyranny, nor from the dominion of deadly superstition, or a still more deadly infidelity. The spot, whether it be beneath a tree

EMANCIPATION OAK

or no, whereon a man ordained by heaven pledges his life to slay an evil or promote a good becomes classic ground. Is there no 'oak of the strong resolve' under which a youthful child of God will put on the whole armour of the Spirit, and go forth to war in the name of the Lord?

Now and again Town Court, Orpington, was visited. Here Mr. Allison, one of Mr. Spurgeon's closest friends, and a deacon at the Tabernacle, lives. Intimation having been given that the pastor was coming, every preparation was made for a warm and hospitable welcome. Visits to Town Court are as refreshing and pleasant in my recollection as any I ever made with Mr. Spurgeon. The man who was capable of 'infinite jest,' and yet who ever exhibited the most remarkable sanctity, was here absolutely at his case, and made the hours spent in lively and pleasant chat pass all too quickly away. On several occasions Mr and Mrs. Allison invited all the students of the Pastors' College to spend a day's holiday with them. This was usually at the commencement of the autumn session. Mr. Spurgeon was, of course, himself present, and during the day gave an address on some important subject relating to Christian ministry.

A mile or two beyond Orpington are the six villages of the *Crays*, which take their name from the delightful little stream upon whose banks they stand. Originally the Cray was called *Grecea*, the Greek for Cray. At St. Paul's Cray Mr. W. Nash has a charming little retreat. Mr. Nash was married by Mr. Spurgeon to Miss Alice Higgs, a daughter of the late Mr. William Higgs, of Brixton; he is, moreover, a deacon of the Baptist Church at Foot's Cray. He was devotedly attached to Mr. Spurgeon, and deeply interested in all his work. It was not to be wondered at, therefore, that Mr. Spurgeon should now and again pay his two friends Mr. and Mrs. Nash a visit. Hither, through an almost endless succession of pleasant landscapes and quiet, pretty Kentish villages, have we driven together, and found the rural restfulness of the surroundings very congenial to the spirit.

Now and again Mr. Spurgeon and the students were invited for the day by the Baptist Church at Loughton, Essex. After luncheon several addresses were given by the president and others, and then the company, numbering nearly one hundred, were treated to a drive through the lovely glades of Epping Forest. Mr. Spurgeon used to enjoy the wild luxuriance of the forest vegetation and its 'boundless continuity of shade' immensely; and his brief addresses given before returning home were among the happiest the students were privileged to hear. He paid visits at different times to colleges near London, but I was never with him upon any of these occasions, although I have had not a few testimonies as to the delight he afforded both tutors and students, who seldom otherwise heard him.

Upon one occasion, I think in the year 1875, Mr. Spurgeon preached at Nantwich and Chester. I was then pastor of a church in Derbyshire, but took a holiday in Cheshire to enjoy hearing him. I

TOWN COURT, OPRINGTON

was invited to spend an evening with him and the late Hugh Stowel Brown, of Liverpool. Mr. Brown possessed much that was after Mr. Spurgeon's own heart. He was remarkable for his robust and manly character; deeply devout also he was, and greatly interested in the welfare of the Kingdom of Christ and the cause of truth. It was no ordinary pleasure to hear these two giants of the pulpit talk on subjects than which to me there could have been none introduced so instructive and fascinating. That very much of pleasant humour and sparkling wit added to the charm of the conversation goes without saying, for while to Mr. Spurgeon would be conceded the palm as a humorist, yet Mr. Brown was a good second. Upon this occasion he greatly delighted Mr. Spurgeon with his droll remarks, dry fun, and comical stories. I used to hear Mr. Brown as a youth at the village chapel near my home, and afterwards occasionally at Chester, and he struck me as being a most remarkable expository preacher. But, like Mr. Spurgeon, he had in him a wondrous blending of the humorous and devout. The evening I spent with these two good men is never likely to pass out of memory.

'I am going to Scotland for a holiday. I should very much like you, friend Williams, to go with me. Will you?' My reader needs not to have any record of my reply. The request was as welcome 'as the liquid lapse of fountain to the thirsty traveller.' I had never seen Scotland, and the prospect of a holiday in a region so famed, among many other things, for its delightful scenery, opened up enchanting expectations of delight. But the realisation exceeded my expectations. The morning we were to start we met at the Tabernacle and drove to St. Pancras Station, and travelled that day to Glasgow. Along the route Mr. Spurgeon pointed out objects of interest, or spoke of events in English history associated with the portion of country through which we journeyed. At Normanton, Mr. Duncan, with whom we were to stay, joined us. We tarried for the night at St. Enoch's Hotel, and left early the next morning for Mr. Duncan's mansion, Benmore, delightfully situated a few miles from the Clyde, and midway between the Holy Loch and Loch Eck. It will be interesting to the reader to see what Mr. Spurgeon himself wrote concerning this reposeful paradise among the hills:

Perhaps some friends may like to see the place of our usual summer retreat. Here dwells our generous friend James Duncan, Esq., and here for many summers he has given us the boon of change of scene, fresh air, quietude, and rest. The sermons on the lawn in front of the house have proved a pleasant labour of love; it has stirred one's heart to see the thousands flocking into that out of the way place to hear the Gospel, and, better still, to mark the devout attention of the assembled multitudes. But our great object has been to let the brain lie fallow, that it may not refuse a harvest in due season. Here we can 'go into the desert and rest awhile.' Out of doors there are all sorts of refreshment for the wearied mind-noble scenery, well-stocked gardens, rivers, lochs, glens, mountains, and woods; and when it rains-and it does in Scotland occasionally - there is a great picture gallery, about as large as the Tabernacle, where Art displays her priceless treasures. Surrounded with affectionate kindness, and enjoying perfect repose, we can have no better opportunity of recovering mental vigour; though, alas! even this cannot ward off the attacks of hereditary disease. Yet, as we sometimes groan in pain, we will also sing in mercy, and bless the Lord, who has dealt so graciously with us.

Sailing down the Clyde for the first time from the pier at Greenock on a perfect summer's morning is an experience which produces so vivid and impressive a picture on the mind that, if other natures are like mine, it will abide for many a year to come. The beautiful expanse of sunlit water, the grand heights of the Argyllshire hills in the distance, with little villages and towns nestling at their base, the fair Loch Long stretching away to the east, with the giant Ben Lomond looming in the distance, and the picturesque Holy Loch lying leisurely towards the north, afford as fair a panorama of natural loveliness as one could ever wish to see. I felt the scene to be 'strangely fair.' We landed at Blairmore, where a carriage was waiting to convey us to our host's hospitable dwelling. Passing through Strone we halted at Strone House, to spend a little while with Mrs. Moubray, Mr. Duncan's sister. Her esteem for Mr. Spurgeon was very great, while for her, because of both ability of mind and nobility of character, he ever cherished the highest admiration and Christian affection. If of Mr. Duncan he could write 'Gaius, mine host,' of his sister he could say, 'She hath been a succourer of many, and of myself also' (Rom. xvi. 2).

With Benmore and its surroundings the reader can readily imagine I was charmed and inspired.

> The sunshine on my path
> Was to me a friend. The swelling hills,
> Or quiet dells retiring far between,
> With gentle invitation to explore
> Their windings, were a calm society
> That talked with me, and soothed me. Then the chant
> Of birds, and chime of brooks, and soft carcass
> Of the fresh sylvan air, made me forget
> All thoughts that broke my peace.

We had not been at Benmore more than an hour or so when Mr. Spurgeon and I wandered off into a wood, and sitting down on the stump of a tree tried to praise God by singing a hymn together. I am sure there was more praise of heart than music of mouth. If singing alone, I can generally employ portions of three or four tunes to one verse; and perhaps on this occasion the fault was mine; but neither of us could keep time; it was a part song, but which part was done the better I will not attempt to judge. The singing gave place to smiling, and then he described the singing in his grandfather's chapel. The old gentleman only had one tune, a common metre, and he used to make a long metre hymn go to this common metre tune by putting an extra 'Um! ah!' at the end of each line.

It is not easy to write of subsequent hours and days we spent together where Lochs 'lay sleeping in the arms of Beauty,' amid the seclusion of mountain fastness, and of valleys and glens; where the splash of the leaping salmon, the screech of the wild-fowl, the lowing of the highland cattle on the hills, or the distant barking of a fox in the woods were almost the only sounds which fell upon our ears. A rush of fragrant and precious memories crowd in upon me as I relive in spirit without effort those seasons, never more to return. I dare not say, as one of our songs has it, that 'Memory is the only friend that Grief can call her own;' but when my dear president and friend was no longer here, Memory proved a friend indeed to Grief, as she recalled those sunny seasons in my life when God seemed to have given me all the blessedness which the beauties of Nature and the charms which the noblest friendship could afford.

In the foreground of our picture of Benmore is a stag lying majestically (as though Benmore belonged to him) with head erect in the meadow. There is a little incident connected with this stag which I think is worth relating. It may tell a 'wee' bit against the writer, but it illustrates Mr. Spurgeon's love of fun. Soon after we were settled down at Benmore, Mr. Duncan said to me, 'Can you shoot, Mr. Williams?' 'Yes,' I replied; 'I was almost born with a gun in my hand.' 'Well, then,' said he, 'I will send to Glasgow for a gun licence for you tomorrow.' I had not specially noticed the stag in the meadow, for there were plenty of deer close too. The next evening, just as it was getting a little dusk, as Mr. Spurgeon, Mr. Duncan, and I were sitting just outside the house, Mr. Spurgeon said, 'Oh, Mr. Williams, I have asked and obtained permission from Mr. Duncan for you to shoot that fine stag in the meadow; see he is lying there now. But you are to shoot him as he lies, for if you get him to move you won't hit him, and Mr. Duncan says you can have a haunch of his venison to take home with you, if you kill him. Now, there is a chance for you!' I expostulated, and said it was not fair to shoot at the animal *sitting*; if I were allowed first to make him rise, I would fire. 'No, no,' said Mr. Spurgeon, 'if you don't shoot him sitting, Mr. Duncan is sure you won't shoot him at all. He is a very unusual sort

BENMORE

of stag.' I yielded, and crept quietly behind the trees in front of him until I got within forty yards of the animal, when, dusk as it was, I began to be suspicious, and soon discovered the *stag was bronze*. I did not fire, or the reader might be now looking at the singular phenomenon of a lively-looking stag's body without a head. I turned round to find Mr. Spurgeon laughing with all his might. A tougher piece of venison than I should have liked to bring to London was that stately monarch of the meadow.

I had some shooting, however. The first day of August arrived, and I was informed 'duck shooting commences today; would I like to go for an hour or two?' I of course said I should. 'The keeper,' a Scot of the first order, accompanied me. 'I hope you won't do as M. Doré did, sir,' was the first greeting I received from him. 'Who's he?' I said. 'Why, the gentleman who painted the fine pictures in the gallery. He stayed here, and went out shooting with me with that gun you've got. He no sooner saw a hare than he began to run after her; and run he did with his gun full cock until she had got out of his reach, and then he fired.' *'Purn, sir! purn!'* I thought the man exclaimed, but could not imagine what he meant. It sounded like *Heron*, and led one to look up; but in much less time than it takes to pen these words I found myself up to the neck, with my gun double cock, in a brook. 'Oh, sir! I warned ye of the *burn*; ye didn't heed me.' The brook was covered with grass and weeds, and I did not suspect danger; between bog and burn there seemed no distinction to me; but the practised eye of the keeper saw it, and warned me, although, alas! in vain. That *burn* will be remembered by the *chill* it gave me. The noble fellow acted splendidly, and soon got me on 'terra cotta,' as the old woman once said on landing. He wanted to change some of his clothes for mine. I declined. He had an extra pair of socks in his game bag. I accepted his offer of these, and shot for the day, and we carried home in the evening a really good bag. Upon reaching Benmore I found Mr. Spurgeon had been working hard most of the day. He was rather concerned as to my brook episode; but the hard walking all day and a hot bath in the evening kept me from taking any harm.

In recent years it has dawned upon me that the keeper had only blank cartridges in his gun when we first began shooting, to test my ability; for he missed every shot; while a little later in the day, when he saw I was not quite a novice with the gun, he brought down nearly every bird he shot at. I am afraid that we preachers sometimes fire blank cartridges. Not only powder but shot is needed, if we are to do real execution. Let any preacher reading these pages turn to William Arthur's *Tongue of Fire*, and he will see what is meant better than any words of mine could tell him.

I slept in the room that Gustave Doré had occupied. I am sorry to say, however, that I found no inspiration of the marvellous genius of the artist left to inspire me. One good story of Gustave Doré I did hear, however, which has served me many a good turn in preaching since. I told it in my volume of *Upton Chapel Sermons*, and many have used it since; but I believe I was the first to give it to the public. Here it is as I had it almost first hand at Benmore, where M. Doré often used to stay. 'When Gustave Doré was painting the face of Christ in one of his pictures, a lady friend came into his studio and began gazing most intently at the face, almost completed. As she was gazing, the artist retired from the picture to one corner of the room, and looked at the face of his friend as eagerly as she looked at the face on the canvas. Turning round she said, "M. Doré, why do you look at me so anxiously?" "I wanted to watch," said he, "the impression that face produced upon yours, and I think you like it." "Yes, I do," she said, "and do you know what I was thinking? - that you could not paint the face of Christ like that unless you loved Him." "Unless I loved Him!" said Doré, agitated. "Well, I trust I do, and that sincerely; but as I love Him more, I shall paint Him better."' I spoke to one at Benmore who knew Doré better perhaps than most people. Many kind things were said of him; but the fear was expressed that, while he had great admiration for the character of Christ, there was not much of heart trust in Him. He loved his mother with rare affection, and gave himself to her with singular devotion; but whether he was one who loved 'mother more than Me,' we must leave the All-wise, All-loving One to judge. It has been a source of regret that I never met Doré; I seem to have been within very close touch of him upon several occasions, but to look into his face or shake his hand was never my privilege.

A select company of friends were invited one evening to meet Mr. Spurgeon. Amongst the guests was Principal Cairns, and after a while he retired with Mr. Spurgeon into the picture gallery for a chat. I was present with these two gracious men. It was a treat indeed to hear their talk. The Churches of Scotland, so far as I remember, were the chief topic of conversation. The talk on the influence of Chalmers and the heroism of the men of the Disruption period occupied not a little of the time. Then the character and work of Candlish, of Thomas Guthrie, of the Bonars, were the subjects of quiet discourse. The state of religion in the Highlands; the decay of doctrinal preaching in the cities; the prospect of the Churches as judged from the colleges; and the question of Disestablishment were also matters dwelt upon. But the Principal ever and anon reverted to Mr. Spurgeon's own great work and influence, upon which, however, he seemed very disinclined to say much. The most vivid and abiding impression of that evening in the picture gallery, however, is of the saintliness of the spirit of that honoured Principal. How gracious his talk was! Mr. Spurgeon spoke of him afterwards with great admiration. Since then, through the hospitable kindness of Mrs. Moubray, I have had the honour of spending a little season at Aberfeldy with the late Andrew Bonar. I can never forget it. I have been a good deal in Scotland of late years, and my estimate of her ministers is a very high one; while of such men as Principal Cairns and Andrew Bonar I feel I can only speak with the most reverent admiration and profound esteem. Scotland has had many an Enoch who has walked with God; and I believe Principal Cairns and Andrew Bonar were of the number. When I first entered college I read the marvellous Memoir of McCheyne, and, as many another, shall feel indebted to it for life; and when in talking to Bonar, and grasping his hand, I remembered I was talking to one whose eyes had seen the face and whose hand had grasped the hand of McCheyne, I realised a sensation peculiarly thrilling and sacred.

The picture gallery, which was, as Mr. Spurgeon says, 'about as large as the Tabernacle,' afforded never-failing interest. Its walls were eloquent indeed with the productions of many masters in the art of portraying all that is most beautiful in earth and sea and sky; and in delineating all that is most expressive in human form and face. On certain days in each week the public were admitted to the gallery free of charge, and thousands of visitors to Argyllshire must retain pleasing and instructive recollections of what once their eyes gazed upon in the gallery at Benmore. Yet to none can the memory be more impressive than to those who day after day quietly and leisurely studied individually those art treasures with Mr. Duncan himself as the instructive guide, and Mr. Spurgeon as a fellow-admirer. Into this picture gallery we generally retired for an hour or two each evening for a chat. My own contribution to the evening was, at the request of Mr. Spurgeon, generally a recitation or a story. I gave one evening several eloquent paragraphs, from Mr. Spurgeon's early sermons, which he did not recognise as his own productions, but which he seemed greatly to enjoy. Another evening I gave *The Burials Bill*, by George R. Sims, a Bill which the Bishop of Lincoln said involved the most serious consequences to the clergy of England, and might imperil the existence of the National Church. Mr. Spurgeon said he wished every Englishman could know this poem.

One evening a gentleman, a friend of Mr. Duncan, was with us: he was staying the night. He had travelled in well-nigh every land, and having a very observant mind he was able to entertain us with descriptions of the geographical peculiarities of the countries through which he had journeyed, also of their institutions, political state, and relationships, and of their condition commercially. Then Mr. Duncan spoke of several of them as they stood in respect to arts and sciences, of their knowledge of chemistry, botany, and astronomy, and as to the prospects of Free Trade with some of them. Then Mr. Spurgeon took up the subject from the religious standpoint, and spoke of the religious beliefs and conditions and customs of these different people. He said: 'A Russian is apt to be superstitious, but he possesses the faith faculty to a high degree, and can believe; but the Germans are far too critical: they lack the faith faculty largely, and are too sceptically inclined: they have given us much we could have done better without. If you could cut a Russian in half, and a German in half, and change the pieces, you might make an almost perfect man of both of them.' The clock pointed to the hour of two before we retired, but I could have sat wide-awake until daylight dawned. One who was present said to me, 'I have learned more to-night than I ever did in any whole year of my life.'

The morning following this talk about the nations Mr. Spurgeon was up quite early, and retired after breakfast to spend the morning on *The Treasury of David*. He asked me to go with him to his study. The Psalm he was expounding was the hundred and twenty-first, beginning, 'I will lift up mine eyes unto the hills, from whence cometh my help.' He greatly enjoyed his work. In his preface to a work written soon after he first came to London he says, 'Writing is to me the work of a slave. It is a delight, a joy, a rapture, to talk out one's thoughts in words that flash upon the mind at the instant when they are required; but it is poor drudgery to sit still and groan for thoughts and words without succeeding in obtaining them.' But he afterwards writes, 'I have some hopes that it may yet be a pleasure to me to serve God with the pen as well as the lip.' These hopes, thus early entertained, were realised; for he found positive delight in the laborious task of expounding the Psalter. Upon this occasion, however, he had most inspiring surroundings and suggestive scenery to help his meditations. As he finished a sheet of his paper he said, 'There, friend, correct and revise that;' but I gave him the poet's words about 'painting the lily,' and only read for my own delight from the written page what thousands have since read from the printed one.

A party of us went one morning to fish in Loch Ech. He and I, however, stayed on shore to kindle a fire, and get the pot boiling, in which we were to cook the salmon; for we were to have a picnic. As we waited for the fisherman to arrive with 'the panting monsters of the flood,' and for which a very warm reception was already prepared, we sat down on the boulder of a projecting rock. He began to instruct me concerning lochs and hills, valleys and mountains; of geological formations and glacial periods when great masses of ice fell in frozen avalanches and scooped out the channels, when the placid lochs rested in their secluded loveliness. He touched upon an uncertainty as to the probable date and duration of glacial periods, but of the certainty of them from the evidence Nature still presents over the northern and southern portions of each hemisphere. Then he said, 'Give me a text, Williams, and I will preach you a sermon.'

His talk had made me feel so unutterably small, as Mr. Archibald Brown has told me it often did him, that I felt prompted to say, by feeling how poor and dim was my light as compared with the lustre of his mind and soul, 'One star differeth from another star in glory.' At once he began to speak of the glory of the stars, and of the 'star depths,' of the special glory of certain single stars, and then of separate constellations of them, giving in each case their names and their position in the heavens, while I, listening with wonder and delight, wished I could only take his sermon down. Then he spoke of the stars as symbols of government, as patterns of constancy, as sources of influence. His finish up of this extempore sermon before his audience was specially fine. 'But,' said he, 'the most glorious of all the stars the heavens ever knew was the Star of Bethlehem. That star led men to Jesus, and anything, any man, doing that shines with a lustre peculiarly Divine.'

'He is the greatest talker living,' said a writer in one of our influential weekly papers; and he was great as a gracious talker as well as in so many other respects. Three or four matters excited my wonder at this time, his humility and great brotherliness - he seemed to treat me as though I had been his equal - his marvellous knowledge of the subject of astronomy: he seemed as familiar with the stars as a schoolmaster with the alphabet: the felicitous ease of his utterance, that there and then, without the inspiration of an audience, he could let flow such a silver stream of language, and clothe his words in such scarlet of eloquence; and last, but most of all, the masterly way in which he made his subject converge and melt into the never-ending theme of his mighty ministry, *Jesus Christ the Saviour of men.*

In leaving the subject of our holiday at Benmore, I am leaving also many a scene undescribed, many incidents unrecorded. Each day was crowded with events. In quiet walks, in delightful picnics, in pleasant drives, there was ever that which kept the mind awake and the heart bright. Mr. Duncan did everything that thoughtful love and a generous heart could suggest to give restful delight to his grateful and illustrious friend, for whose sake I was thus also privileged. This my first visit to Scotland secured for me many subsequent ones. I have since then preached in many of her places of worship, and cruised for weeks together with some of her worthiest ministers along her western shores, on to Ireland, and away to Oban, Staffa, Iona, and Stornaway, exploring on our journey all scenes of inspiring memory or of special beauty. But another volume would be needed to write of our subsequent pleasures on slimmer seas in Scotland.

An hour or so before we left Benmore for home Mr. Spurgeon came suddenly on me as I was counting some coins I had in my hands. 'Hullo!'' he said, 'counting out your money? What are you going to do?' 'I was going to give something to two or three of the servants,' I said. 'How much?' I told him. 'Yes, that will do well, and there is the money for you.' I demurred taking it. He would have no denial. Yet it was just like him. While he was ever a careful spender of money, he was ever a generous giver of it. He greatly admired generosity in others too, and exemplified the grace himself. After a sermon he preached on Mr. Duncan's lawn the hearers placed about 80*l*. in two great flower vases as a gift to the Stockwell Orphanage, which greatly cheered his heart. I once heard him say, 'Some people's pockets are hermetically sealed, like the tins of Australian meat, and you cannot get even a smell at them.' But for generous givers, beloved of God, no word of praise was too great.

Our journey home was without any special incidents, except that by this time the papers had given the information that Mr. Spurgeon was in Scotland, and that he was expected to return south on a certain day, which brought groups of people to several stations who were anxious to see him, and on the part of some to, if possible, have a few words.

CHAPTER V

THE PEERLESS PRESIDENT

THE Pastor' College was the first philanthropic institution Mr. Spurgeon founded, and to the last it was dearer to his heart than any other, for the opportunity it afforded of extending the Saviour's kingdom in saving the souls of men.

The members of the Conference were on one occasion streaming into Kingsgate Street Chapel for the inaugural Conference when a stranger asked if it was a meeting of the Royal College of Surgeons. 'No, sir,' replied one of the brethren, 'but of the Royal College of Spurgeons.' The President expressed the hope that each man would seek to be right royal in character and service, and thus prove the college to be, what he believed it was, his most royal service for the Master. To no work did he give himself with more absolute consecration of money and mind and heart than to the training of his men for the Christian ministry; and in the judgment of not a few of the ministers educated in his college the splendour of his ability and the greatness of his character were more conspicuous as President than either as author or preacher. In the pulpit, looking down upon a sea of upturned faces while his charming voice made human hearts beat and throb under the spell of the old, old story, he

A GROUP OF STUDENTS AT THE PASTORS' COLLEGE

was ever great; as the orphan's friend, surrounded with groups of happy children, whose faces were always sunniest and voices most cheery when their foster-father was with them, he was indeed great; but in the college and at the Conference, filling with the enthusiasm and inspiration of God men who were to carry the Gospel to hundreds of thousands of their fellow men, he ever seemed to us greatest of all. There, more than anywhere, his sparkling wit, his overmastering oratory, his felicity of illustration, his almost endless resources of material, and his intense love to God and men proved him to be a genius of the first order, a Christian of the loftiest type, and a President peerless in wit and power to thrill and inspire, and in his wisdom to counsel and guide Christian ministers.

In the presence of his students he seemed to be as much at home, and as free from all restraints, as in the quiet seclusion of his own home. Many a time when listening to him in college I felt that the world outside, having only his works or having heard him preach, did not know Spurgeon. There were elements and powers in him which only those who saw him often in his presidential chair were acquainted with. In the pulpit, as he himself has said, there was often the necessity to repress certain tendencies of his nature, such as wit, sarcasm, and mimicry; but in the college these were allowed full play, so that his talks were not more instructive than they were entertaining and amusing. The absolute *humanness* of the man too was seldom seen as in college. If each student had taken notes of his wise and witty utterances, Dr. Pierson's remarks would prove to be most true. He says: 'If the history of his humour alone could be written, it would fill volumes, and it would be a great contribution to the innocent merriment of the human race as well as a great revelation of character. He had an anecdote for any and every new emergency, and many of his stories carried all the force of argument and illustration combined.' Some of his smart sayings thought to be original were doubtless borrowed, for he possessed an almost unique collection of books on fun, humour, and proverbial philosophy. He told the students to beg, borrow, or steal their illustrations from any and every source, and that he thus obtained many of his funny sayings is beyond question. But for the most part his wit was as really original and spontaneous as it was chaste, keen, and strong, and nowhere was it more manifested than in the presence of his students. One reason why the President was generally so 'colloquial' familiar, full of anecdote, and often humorous,' was the fact that he met the students at the end of the week, and, as he himself says, 'I find them weary with sterner studies, and I judge it best to be as lively and interesting in my prelections as I well can be. They have had their fill of classics, mathematics, and divinity, and are only in a condition to receive something which will attract and secure their attention and fire their hearts.' That he expected each student to give his whole heart to the 'sterner studies' the following letter, sent to one whose application to enter college is thus accepted, will show.

Westwood, Beulah Hill, Upper Norwood
May 20, 1889

DEAR SIR, - Come to college August 6, and may the Lord prove that this is according to His mind. Come to work hard, and to pray harder. May you be a willing plodder and a great soul-winner.

Yours very truly,
C. H. SPURGEON

It would be unfair and unwise to report many of his college sayings; they were meant for the ears of his students only; while with respect to quite a number of them the circumstances or events which gave them birth are needed to enable the reader to understand their piquancy and force. None of his utterances can possibly be read with the interest felt by those who heard them from the President's own lips, and who saw the singular gestures, luminous smiles, and often matchless mimicry associated with their delivery. Yet from among the almost numberless sayings preserved many may be selected, as likely to afford both pleasure and profit to such as care to read them.

Here are a few:

I have often heard of ministers being killed with kindness, but I never yet saw the cemetery where they were buried.

Brethren, it is always better to go where God sends us without question. Jonah was told to go to Nineveh, but he thought he would go to Tarshish; but when the whale got hold of him, he found himself sucked in.

Put plenty into your sermons, gentlemen. After hearing some discourses I have been reminded of the request of the farmer's boy to his missus when eating his broth. 'Missus, I wish you would let that chicken run through this broth once more.'

Adapt your preaching to your audience. Some men seem to throw a harpoon at a herring, and try to catch a whale with a sprat.

Some ministers don't go to sleep in the middle of a sermon - they were not awake when they began.

The perfection of reading in the pulpit is to talk it. Yes, and of preaching too.

Yes, prepare your prayers - but by preparing yourselves.

Don't court controversy; but if you do fight, mind you make the fellow catch it.

We must almost abound in tricks of art in the pulpit to make our preaching take.

How you will need your people's prayers! Ministers have their own and others' troubles heaped upon them.

Don't covet high positions, for wealth is fleeting. Riches and honours soon pass away, but wrestle hard with sin and sinners.

Ignorance of self is ignorance of God.

Look upon your troubles as the shadows of coming mercies.

It is an awkward experience to preach on the Devil and feel full of your subject.

Mind you avoid inappropriate texts. One brother preached on the loss of a ship with all hands on board from, 'So He bringeth them to their desired haven,' and another returning from his marriage holiday, 'The troubles of my heart are enlarged. Oh! bring me out of my distresses.'

Mind your illustrations are correct. It will never do to describe Noah as one did, sitting outside the Ark reading his Bible.

Always get the true meaning of a text. One local preacher took for his text 'He for our profit,' and preached on 'the prophetical office of Christ.'

Let your illustrations at least be tolerably fresh. That one about the ship being lost and one of the crew being saved by a lifeboat, and whispering, 'There's another man, there's another man!' What good can be done by so worn out an illustration - except to give some old maids fresh hope?

No minister will so minister to a minister as Augustine.

The master minds of Church history are not many. You may take a step from Paul to Augustine, then from Augustine to Calvin, and then - well, you may keep your foot up for a good while before you find such another.

Let your sermons be such that you can feed on them as you preach them, like the Abyssinians, who will ride a bullock and cut a beef-steak as they go.

Scott's *Commentary* will not help you much. Don't give your people too many of these Scottish notes.

Napoleon succeeded because there was a little Napoleon in every Frenchman.

Every sermon should be the man in flower.

A preacher should be borne away by the force of the truth he preaches.

Be determined to succeed. If you have great difficulties, cut your way with the diamond of faith.

Let the spirit of prayer perfume all these college rooms.

The twin names of God are Light and Love.

Mind your figures of speech are not cracked. Don't talk like the brother who said, 'I fly from star to star, from cherry-*beam* to cherry-*beam*.' Nor like the temperance orator who said, 'Shoulder your axes, brethren, and let us plough the sea, that the ship of temperance may sail o'er the land.' Nor yet like the Irish politician who said, 'There is ill brooding o'er Ireland. I smell a rat - I see it floating in the air - I nip it in the bud.'

The Church of the time and the Church for the time may be very different.

Don't begin an enterprise you have not some prospects of carrying out. George III. wanted to build a marble palace, but he has only left us a Marble Arch. He was a sovereign who was in want of sovereigns.

Seek to develop your whole character. A student who grows lopsided will never make an all-round minister.

In speaking be natural, for if you are not B natural you will be A flat. Let every man speak after his kind. If Dr. Parker were to speak like a young lady, he would not speak after his kind.

Get Bates' *Encyclopaedia of Illustrations.* Too expensive, did you say? Well, make a present of it all round, then each man will get it for nothing.

Here is a riddle for you. 'If Paul was the least of all saints, what size are you?'

If God intends a man for the ministry; He gives him ability. When one applies to come into college with a head no larger than an exaggerated pimple, and who in speaking has to say, 'Wound the wagged wocks the wagged waskles wan,' I know he was never intended for a preacher.

To be effective preachers you must be sound theologians. Be sure you read Owen, Charnock, and Augustine.

Priests usurp the prerogative of Christ, and then call us Korah, Dathan, and Abiram; but they are they.

London is the most Christian city in the world, and yet a solid mass of sin. Pray for London.

Though you are teetotallers, you must all come to your bier at last.

Mind you keep your prayer meetings up. I would rather they should be a kind of celestial free-and-easy than the dull things some are.

Long prayers injure prayer meetings. Fancy a man praying for twenty minutes, and then asking God to forgive his shortcomings.

Every improvement in virtue will mean advancement in happiness.

Make large demands on infinite love.

The Primitive Methodists used to say they did not want any D.D.'s, because their theology was never sick. If any of you get A.M., mind it does not mean, After Money.

We deprive souls of a privilege when we don't make a collection.

The Song of Songs is in the very centre of the Bible, as the Holy of Holies in the sanctuary.

One secret of Solomon's wanderings was that he was not afflicted. This covenant mark he lacked.

Never parley with Temptation. If he gets you on debatable ground, the Devil gains.

God gives some good things to all men, but all good things to some men.

I will decide as the colonists of Connecticut did; they said they would be guided by the laws of God until they had time to make better.

The key word of the Epistle to the Hebrews is *better*. Christ is better than the angels, and better than Moses. Then there are better promises and a better covenant. You might preach on these betters, then you would preach better every time.

Some men only shine like the moon, when they ought to burn like the sun.

Young ministers are generally despised by people who wish they were young themselves.

Why, the very spelling of the Devil's name shows what he is - Devil, evil, vile, ill, hell !

Don't worry about originality, brethren; Christ never claimed it. He says: 'The words that I speak are not Mine, but His that sent Me.' The Holy Spirit did not claim it, for it is written, 'He shall not speak of Himself, but whatsoever He shall hear, that shall He speak.' In fact, the only original thinker and speaker in the Bible is he of whom it is written, 'When he speaketh a lie, he speaketh of his own.'

We need to be as simple as if we were preaching to asses, as indeed we often do. An old farmer, after listening to a sermon on 'The fool hath said in his heart, There is no God,' said to the preacher, 'I believe there is a God after all, though your sermon was very clever.'

'The son of Amram stood unmoved!' 'Who was he?' inquired the critic. 'Moses.' 'Then why didn't you say so?'

Get amongst your people, or somebody may be saying of you as one old lady said of her minister - that he was invisible all the week and incomprehensible on the Sunday.

'Why did the eunuch go on his way rejoicing?' asked the teacher. 'Because Philip had a-done a-preaching to him, sir,' said the boy.

Those who are always preaching on Daniel and Revelation I regard as subjects for admiration rather than imitation. Don't be ambitious to become a *Cumming* tribulation preacher.

Be 'High Calvary preachers,' as one described certain high-doctrine brethren. A minister should be able to say that word *grace* in his sleep.

Shun all affectation in the pulpit: some preachers seem to think it a means of grace for people to see them blow their nose. As for being weeping ministers - miserable waste of salt water. And mind you never get into the goody-goody style. One of this sort said, 'I was reading this morning in *dear Hebrews.*'

Mind the theme of your sermon suits yourself. A beardless boy should not preach from, 'I have been young, and now am old.'

Mind you keep growing, brethren. Everyone of you should feel that there is a bigger man inside of you. Mind that you have big hearts. Let your hearts be like some great harbour, where multitudes of souls can come for anchorage and rest. Get bigger heads too. You can never get much out of them if you don't first put it in. Let them grow until they crack if you like, and then you can get more into them. Have any of you heard your heads crack yet?

Thoughts belong to everybody, brethren. I must not wonder if other people steal my thoughts, since I have stolen so many of other people's. For my part I beg, borrow, and steal from every conceivable quarter; *but* when I steal a man's coat, I tear it all to pieces and make a waistcoat of it.

If when you get into a pastorate you take matters as easily as an old shoe, the Devil will soon make a slipper of you. An idle minister is a detestable object.

Don't give yourselves to too much courting. You won't find it any easier to fight the Devil with a girl on your arm. You will think, 'I don't need to study! O you angel in pink and blue, with blue eyes! Oh! I wish we were married.' ... Fill the reservoir!

Keep to your topic in your sermon; you can't have every subject in one discourse. Some put too much into a sermon; it is a field of corn, not bread; a load of bricks, but not a house.

'I am wandering in my mind,' said one. 'Well,' said a friend, 'you won't go far.' Keep from wandering in your preaching, or your great minds might lead you far astray. An occasional ramble may not hurt. Vary your work by studying to stick to your subject.

Beware of your h's. One friend read, 'Many there be which go in their *h*at,' and another, '*H*it *h*is I ; be not afraid.' Be careful of your emphasis also. One read, 'He said unto his sons, Saddle me the ass; so they saddled *him.*'

If you want God to bless your preaching, you must put plenty of Gospel into it. I have heard a minister pray at the close of a sermon, 'Lord, convert some by this sermon,' when there wasn't enough

Gospel in it to convert a periwinkle.

Have regular hours for study. You will find that whatever hours you choose you will have most visitors just then - the Devil will see to that.

In studying your subject be like a mouse in a Cheshire cheese - bore a hole right through it; you will fatten as you go.

If you want to be good speakers, talk often. None talk more sweetly than the ladies, because they are always at it.

The *Daily News* says that my sermon last Sunday morning was not at all striking. I did not try to strike anybody - I wanted to feed the sheep.

In addressing the new students I shall divide my words of greeting into two divisions: First, you're a fool. Second, you are not the only one here.

Upon several occasions Mr. Spurgeon said that the first lesson a student learned was that he was a fool, and the second that there were several others about him.

Some neglect the gift that is in them because they are so busy in looking after the gift that is in somebody else.

Don't build arguments on metaphors. A man said to me the other day, 'You should not talk of sects, Mr. Spurgeon. A sect is impossible, because a sect means a section, and you can't have a section of the Bride of Christ. Fancy a section of a bride!' I said, 'My friend, I'll think over that idea. By the way, I was grieved to hear you have been guilty of cannibalism.' 'What do you mean?' said he. 'Why, I mean this; you eat mutton chops, and don't you know we are all the Lord's sheep?'

Study your Bible in a common-sense way, brethren; read on, and get into the spirit and meaning of verse, chapter, or book. The way some people study it reminds me of flea catching: they pick a thought up here, then over the leaves go, and they are after another there, and holding it between thumb and finger they cry, 'Here it is, I've got it. Does not this precious verse teach so and so?' and then they go deluding souls and building up false systems with that sort of thing.

Don't write poetry, gentlemen, if you can help it. There may come to you, as there do to most people, weak moments when you cannot help it. Well, write away, and then - well, burn it. Do you know the difference between poetry and blank verse? My work as editor of our magazine puts me in a position to tell you:

> I went to the mill dam
> And in I fell jam.

That is poetry, gentlemen.

> I went to the mill dam
> And in I fell flop.

Gentlemen, that is blank verse.

Whitfield is said to have read Matthew Henry's *Commentary* through on his knees. I think it would have done him more good if he had read it sitting in an easy chair. I hope each brother will read Henry through the first year of his ministry. It will prove a life-long blessing to him if he does.

Don't imitate the peculiarities of great preachers. Thomas Binney used to pull his thoughts out of the palm of his left hand with two fingers, and very wonderful thoughts they often were. The students of New College, who often heard him, used to try the same dodge, but most of them found the palm of their hand had nothing in it, and so they looked rather ridiculous.

Christ said, 'Feed My sheep ... Feed My lambs.' Some preachers, however, put the food so high that neither lambs nor sheep can reach it. They seem to have read the text, 'Feed My giraffes.'

John Newton said he put Calvinism into his preaching as he put sugar into his tea. Yes, that is the way to teach it, brethren; let your whole ministry be flavoured with these delightful doctrines of grace. And don't be afraid of putting in an extra lump of sugar sometimes. I regard modern thought as a totally new *cult*, having no more relation to the Gospel than the mists of the morning to the everlasting hills.

If God's Word cannot be trusted, then are our harbours turned into whirlpools and our rocks into clouds.

Such quotations might be continued to almost any length. Those given later in the chapter on Table Talk may prove acceptable to not a few. He once told the students that quotable sentences, learned by heart, would prove of great value to them in speaking and preaching. Perhaps his own choice sayings, so pungent and practical, may help to supply some quotable sentences for those who need them. In the meantime it may be agreeable to the reader if the 'plums' are mixed with a little lighter and more easily digested material.

We were frequently treated on Friday afternoons to talks about books, authors, preachers, reformers, and poets. What an omnivorous reader the President must have been! To us it seemed that there was no great book or noted writer of ancient or modern times he was not acquainted with. Theologians, preachers, scientists, philosophers, poets, he knew them all, and in turn would give us accounts of the men and their books, of the times in which they lived and the circumstances under which they wrote. Week by week we were advised what books to buy. To many this advice has proved of almost priceless value. 'He who has not Bishop Hall's *Contemplations*, let him sell his garment to buy it. Hall was a clergyman, nay, worse, he was a bishop; but mind you read him,' was his counsel one Friday. 'Stint yourselves to buy good books; try ever to be improving your stock. The minister's life and library are the people's granary: they always suffer if either of these be low,' was his plea upon another occasion. Often he would give us readings from books we were advised to secure. These readings of his were a special treat, quite as much for the manner as for the matter. Mr. Sheridan Knowles, when lecturer on elocution at Regent's Park College, once heard Mr. Spurgeon speak in that institution, when he was but twenty years of age, and complimented him most highly before the company present on his elocution. It was to each of his own students a lesson in the art of elocution to hear him read, he of course intending it to be so. Those of us who heard him read

Shakespeare can never forget it: his rendering of Antony's oration over the body of Caesar made the scene so realistic to us that we could almost believe we were gazing upon the 'rent the envious Casca made,' and upon the blood which flowed when Brutus 'plucked his cursed steel away.' Although we had readings from Scott, Milton, Cowper, Wordsworth, Coleridge, and many others, I used to think his renderings of Young's *Night Thoughts* was, after Shakespeare, the most impressive. He advised us to read and learn Young. He said he was one of the most quotable of our poets. John Wesley used to carry a copy of Young in the saddle when itinerating through the country. Young himself, however, came in for some strong denunciation, for, while he exhorted his readers to 'other worldliness,' he was constantly scheming for petty preferments in this. Cowper was a special favourite with the President; and singularly sweet and gracious was the influence felt when he, with subdued voice and tender pathos, read from this delightful poet.

It need scarcely be said that we often listened to the reading of sterner stuff than is to be found in any of the poets; but as theological students we were equally thankful to be introduced to Augustine, Owen, Baxter, Brooks, Charnock, Manton, Sibbes, and to a host of other illustrious names, whose writings embraced varied fields of literature and science. Then the lectures delivered covered a very extensive area, and dealt with every conceivable phase of life and experience that bore any relationship to the Christian ministry. We had talks on private and public prayer; on the maintenance of our own spiritual life; on sermons, their matter, the best methods of preparation; on delivery; on the aim and end of preaching, &c. Some few of these are printed in *Lectures to my Students*, and all who read them acknowledge their power and charm. Yet these in print give but a faint indication of the numerous subjects that at one time or another were the theme of his enchanting talk; talk charged with wit and humour, repartee and raillery, anecdote and illustration, mimicry and genuine bursts of oratory, and which filled many an hour with merriment, and sometimes with even boisterous abandon; yet with such merriment and abandon that a closing prayer which carried all spirits into the presence of the Eternal seemed the most harmonious and fitting ending to the afternoon's instruction and delight. The brightest and most stimulating memories of many a minister's life come from the Fridays of their college days.

Now and again students were given subjects upon which they were to speak at once. Great fun was often thus created. One brother was asked to make an impromptu illustration from something in the room. It was very draughty, for the President would ever have plenty of fresh air. The student, raising his coat-collar, said, 'This room is like the Devil, it blows from all quarters.' Another student had for his subject Zacchaeus. He was terribly nervous and could only say, 'Dear brethren, the Bible says Zacchaeus was up a tree. That's where I feel I am. He made haste and came down; that is what I shall now do,' and he sat down. Of one student, who came in for a good deal of chaff, the President said, 'It is unfair of you to make that brother one of the Newington Butts.'

Frequent allusion was made to the subject of courting, and sound and sage advice was given concerning courtship and marriage; advice, I fear, that was not always acted upon. One brother was reported as being engaged to three young ladies at once. One Friday the President called him into his private room, when, to the student's blank astonishment, the three young ladies were present. Mr. Spurgeon gave him a warm five minutes, and bade him there and then make his choice of one of them. The student did so, but with what result I cannot say.

Whenever the President touched on the matter of personal purity he was terribly in earnest. Any swerving from the path of strict rectitude came in for scathing denunciation. I can never forget one Friday when it had been reported to him that a minister in whom he had placed great confidence, and who had gone from the college, had greatly fallen. Rolling up his coat-sleeve, and placing his bare wrist on the platform rail, he said, in tones solemn and awful, 'Brethren, I would sooner have had this right hand severed from my body than that this should have happened.'

The first day after each summer vacation was a field day, and was generally spent at or near Mr. Spurgeon's house, when he lived at Nightingale Lane. A field near was placed at his disposal, in which a tent was erected for dinner and tea. When he went to live at Westwood his own grounds afforded every accommodation necessary. I received an invitation to these festive gatherings, and had the privilege of being at many of them. Mr. G. Holden Pike, who helped Mr. Spurgeon in literary work for many years, and who was admitted to much close intimacy with him, and whom I have frequently met at Westwood, was invariably to be found at these annual gatherings, by the President's request, and in the columns of several weekly papers he recorded much of what was said. I shall not therefore dwell at length upon what has already been described many times over. The meeting in the tent or under the oak tree was really the treat of the day. The welcome given to the new students and the address, directed especially to them, often occasioned much mirth; but they were ever warned not to estimate college life from the festivities of the opening day. Speaking in the tent once with an audience before him which, as he said, *stretched from pole to pole*, the President said:

'Gentlemen, keep to Bible themes in your preaching. Some like to talk of Darwin and Tyndall and Huxley in their sermons: it gives a show of learning, you know. But I like to mention Paul and Peter and Jesus Christ in my sermons; and Darwin and Tyndall and Huxley may go to the -' A slight pause and laughter: 'Brethren, you interrupt me; it is unfair - may go to the - aboriginal monkeys from whence they say they sprang.'

Among the men who assembled at Nightingale Lane field day upon one occasion was one dressed in a little too dandyfied a style for the President's taste. He had on patent boots and light trousers, and amused Mr. Spurgeon by his swellish appearance. The President eyed him, but said nothing, until he proposed to run the brother a race. This was agreed upon, Mr. Spurgeon being given ten yards' start. He had already selected the course, having just before walked over it, and seen a boggy place into which one could sink half-way up to the knees. He was careful in the race to let the man in patent boots pass him just in time to save himself, and to see the brother dash into the mire. No real harm was done, and a good bit of fun was created, while the brother soon understood the meaning of this singular remonstrance.

We met for conference once in a neighbouring chapel while the present college buildings were being erected. One of the pastors called out in the meeting, 'Dear President, where is the site of the new college? We should like to see it before we return.' 'It is in the parson's garden behind the Tabernacle,' was the reply. 'We are going to cultivate it for him to grow Dissenters on.' It speaks volumes for the great esteem in which Mr. Spurgeon was held by all sections of the community that he could thus obtain the freehold of the ground from the Ecclesiastical Commissioners to *grow Dissenters on.* To few others, we think, would such a concession have been made. He said the ground needed no consecration, as it had belonged to the

A LESSON TO A STUDENT

Church.

In conversation with individual men as well as in addressing the students his wit was ever declaring itself 'I did not see you at Conference yesterday,' he said to one. 'No, sir; I came up in the night.' 'Oh! you are like Jonah's gourd, then; I hope you won't perish in a night.' To a Mr. Brown, who had been preaching in Holland for several weeks, he said, 'We shall know you now as Brown Holland.' To a student settling at Deal he said, 'Well, brother, go to Deal and fight the Deil; hit him hard, I owe him no love.' To one going to Barnes he said, 'Don't be like the ravens, they never gather into barns.' In reply to a Church who wanted a man to fill the chapel, he said he had no student big enough for that, but he would send the biggest he had got, and his name was Whale. To several who were going to coal districts in the Midlands he said, 'You fellows ought to blaze away, having so much coal under you.' To Mr. Barley he said, 'You will do all right as long as you keep from getting malted.' To one going to a specially difficult sphere his command was, 'Now stick to it until you have really done something. Hold on with both hands, and if you cannot, then hold on with your finger-nails, and if you cannot do that, then hold on with your eyebrows, but do stick to it.'

My friend and old fellow-student, Mr. Abraham, has supplied me with the four following reminiscences of college days, of which I gladly avail myself:

The unprepared sermon and the interrupting storm. - It has been said by some that Mr. Spurgeon often went into the pulpit without knowing what he was going to preach about; but this is a practice which he always condemned most emphatically, his strong common sense continually insisting that God demanded the preacher's best work and ripest thought. There were times, few and far between, in which he was called upon to speak an unpremeditated word. He had once gone to a service with his sermon well prepared, when he discovered that every idea concerning the selected text had utterly gone from him, while another passage on the opposite page stared at him with eyes of fire. After a struggle to regain the lost sermon he was compelled to face the new text, and obey its command of enforcement. During the hymn before the sermon he saw his way through an introduction and a first division, and for a time all went smoothly. At last he found himself coming to a point beyond which he saw no possibility of progress, and the prayer that went up for help appeared to be in vain. But while uttering the last words that were in his mind a sudden thunderstorm burst upon the place with such fierceness that the preacher's voice was lost in the noise of the elements. After a few minutes the storm cleared, but such an interruption would have made it unadvisable to proceed with the best arranged discourse, and a few words by way of pointing a lesson from the tempest brought the service to a close. Two young men of great usefulness were led to the Saviour on that occasion - one by the unprepared and unfinished discourse, and the other by the words spoken after the storm had passed. His advice to preachers was that they should never undertake so difficult a task unless under equal compulsion.

An unusual method of pulpit preparation. - The following singular experience was related by the President in one of his Friday talks to the students. He had visited the death-bed of a valued member of the Tabernacle, and had received from him a text, with the request that it should be the basis of the sermon for the coming Sunday morning. It was no unusual thing for the great preacher to obtain his messages for the people in this way, and the promise was readily made. To get the sermon out of the text proved to be a task of extraordinary difficulty, and after many fruitless attempts, carried forward until late on the Saturday night, he was advised to retire to rest, with the promise of an early call, and in the hope that in the dawning of the Sabbath the needed light would come. He was not awakened until the usual hour for rising, and began to complain that the promise had been broken, when he was asked to listen to a few notes on the text which were read from manuscript in the reader's hand. With eager delight he exclaimed, 'Why that's the very thing I want! But where did you get it?' He was then informed that *he had preached the sermon during the night while soundly sleeping*, and his congregation of one had acted as his reporter. That sermon was preached on the same day, and the President declared that it went much better than many which had been prepared in his wide-awake hours. But he warned the students that they must not go too often to their dreams for their sermons, as there were dreams enough in most of their sermons already.

A visit from a madman. - In relating a variety of experiences which might come to a preacher, the following story was once given to us. One day a visitor called at Nightingale Lane with a request that he might be allowed to see Mr. Spurgeon at once on urgent business. He was told that an interview could not be had just then, but persistency prevailed. On entering the study the stranger closed the door, stood with his back to it, and began 'What's this you've been telling the people at the Tabernacle about me?' 'Why, nothing, my friend.' 'Oh yes, you have, and I've come to have it out with you. I'm not going to stand this sort of thing.' Seeing that the man was stout and strong, and that he carried a stick like himself, Mr. Spurgeon adopted a soothing, matter of fact, reasoning tone. 'Well, my friend, you are a stranger to me. I don't think I ever saw you before, and certainly I don't know you. If I know nothing about you

I can't tell anything, can I?' 'No,' said the man, 'I suppose you can't' and then, after a meditative pause, asked, 'Have you a brother?' 'Yes.' 'Is he much like you?' 'No, I can't say he is.' Then came a furious burst. 'No, it wasn't your brother, it was you; and I mean to settle the matter. Do you know that *I have been in an asylum*?' 'Have you? I am sorry to hear that.' 'Yes, and when I was there I was so strong that it took ten men to hold me.' The man began to flourish his stick, and make threatening advances, from which there seemed no possibility of escape, and then asked, 'Are you strong?' This was the preacher's opportunity, and power of will over brute strength at once asserted itself. 'Yes, I am terrifically!' 'What, as strong as ten men?' Mr. Spurgeon sprang to his feet, assumed a tragic tone, and shouted, 'Yes, I'm stronger than a hundred men, and if you don't get out of this room I'll crush every bone in your wretched little body!' The man trembled with fear, turned to the door, threw it aside, rushed down the stairs, out through the doorway, and along the road, as if pursued by furies - leaving his stick behind as a memento of his visit. With thankfulness for deliverance, and strict orders that the dangerous visitor should not be allowed to get into his study again, Mr. Spurgeon turned to his work, and was not a little relieved when he heard that the escaped lunatic had been taken back into secure custody. Of course the narrative occasioned much laughter in the college; and the President observed, 'Yes, gentlemen, it's easy for you to laugh, and so it is for me now, but it was no laughing matter at the time.'

The value of a D.D. degree. - It often happened that a distinguished visitor from home or foreign lands would come to the college on a Friday afternoon. I well remember a tall, good-looking Yankee, who was invited by the President to say a few words to the students at the end of the lecture. The speaker referred to the admiration of Americans for our President, and threw a good deal of warmth into his eulogiums. As a brilliant climax to the speech he produced a roll of parchment, and intimated that he had been commissioned from a certain American University *to confer the Doctor of Divinity degree upon Mr. Spurgeon*, and then he begged him to accept the document and the distinction it was intended to impart. The students had the two faces in view at the same moment, and noted the earnest and serious look of the Yankee in contrast to the surprised and amused expression of the President. We knew that something was coming soon. Words of great heartiness and evident sincerity told of the gratification with which the assurances of confidence and regard from across the water were received, and something like this came at the end: 'I'm really much obliged to you, sir, and to the good friends you represent, for all the kind things you have said. I wish I deserved them all, but I am sure that I do not.' Then, as if suddenly recollecting the parchment which lay upon the table, and with a gentle genial humour in the tone which put all rudeness or discourtesy out of the question: 'But as for this - well, to tell you the truth, my dear friend, *I wouldn't give you tuppence for a bushel of 'em!*'

Mr. Spurgeon always felt that a 'D.D.' was a doubtful distinction for himself, whatever glory it might confer upon other men, although there were men for whom he readily recognised its appropriateness. At the close of each Conference Mr. Spurgeon used to invite about a dozen brethren down to his house to spend the afternoon and evening. If the President found it a treat to have them, the ministers found it a treat indeed to spend a few hours there with him. Story-telling, singing, instrumental music, chats upon all manner of subjects, caused the hours to fly swiftly by. Every man felt the privilege to be as a crowning favour to a week of blessing.

CHAPTER VI

TABLE TALK

IF the table talk of Martin Luther and of Samuel Taylor Coleridge deserved to be preserved and printed, we are convinced that the unanimous verdict of such as heard much of Mr. Spurgeon's talk, either in college or elsewhere, will be that his also merited this distinction. It is to be hoped that one day a volume will be given to the public containing some of the many pungent, wise, and gracious sentences to be found in rich abundance in his printed lectures and sermons. We have several volumes of extracts from his works already; but another, made up of his proverbial sayings, choice epigrams, happy sentences bright with wit and luminous with the wisdom which cometh from above, would prove very acceptable and helpful to teachers and speakers in this busy age. In this chapter I restrict myself for the most part to what I personally heard from his own lips, though some few of the things to be recorded may, at one time or another, have been picked up in conversation with others, or from ephemeral literature, where they were likely to be forgotten and buried.

He never said, as has often been reported, 'Resist the Devil, and he will flee from you,' but 'Resist a deacon, and he will fly at you';

but I heard him say of a certain minister, 'If he would only pray with his deacons, he would not so fight with them.' All the Christian Church knows on what terms of loving cordiality he lived with his own deacons. He once said at a public meeting, 'My deacons and elders have no such nonsense in their intercourse with me in calling me "the reverend gentleman"; in fact, they are profane enough to call me "The Governor," and among them there are "Joe," and "Jim,' and lots of such names, all most respectable gentlemen, I assure you. They all ought to be esquires, no doubt, but amongst us there is no squirearchy.'

Speaking of the relationship of minister to deacons he said: 'A minister is to take the oversight of the flock. Deacons are not shepherds, but part of the flock; therefore a minister must take the oversight of his deacons.' He esteemed his own deacons very highly in love for their work's sake. 'Happy am I to have such deacons,' he once said. 'Happier still are they to have such a pastor,' was the reply. In their presence his fun often bubbled up. The following example has been given by another, though I had it first; but for the sequel it deserves to have a place here. 'What tune shall we have to this hymn?' he said to the precentor one day. 'Redditch.' 'Here, friend,' he said to a deacon present, whose hair was inclined to be reddish, 'here is your tune.' 'My hair is not red, but golden,' was the reply. 'Ah! yes, golden,' said the pastor, 'eighteen carat.' The proprietors of a weekly periodical offered a prize of one guinea for the best joke to be sent in on a post-card. I sent the above, and obtained the guinea. Mr. Spurgeon said if I did not give him half of it, he should consider me in his debt at the day of judgment.

The world knows how strongly he opposed Roman Catholicism, as subverting some of the first and most vital principles of the Gospel. One Sunday morning a deacon, since deceased, said to him,

'Last Sunday, sir, I was in France, and as I was seven miles from any Protestant place of worship, I went to the Roman Catholic Mass, and I never felt the presence of God more in this Tabernacle than I did there.' 'Only proves Scripture true,' said the pastor: '"If I make my bed in hell, behold, Thou art there."'

Looking over some books in a second-hand book shop, a Paedobaptist, with questionable taste, pointed to a book in favour of infant baptism, and said, 'Here, Mr. Spurgeon, here is your thorn in the flesh.' 'Finish the quotation, brother - A messenger of Satan to buffet me,' was the smart rejoinder.

He once told the orphan boys to cultivate the art of speaking, and to take encouragement from himself, for when he came into this country he could not speak a word of English. At a meeting of the board of trustees of the Orphanage one day, when the business was concluded he said, in the most grave and solemn tones, 'Before we separate I have a most serious matter to bring before you. It has to do with the Head Master, Mr. Charlesworth. He has introduced a child into the Orphanage without the consent of any of the trustees.' The trustees were astonished, and their countenances assumed very serious aspects. Questions were asked, great surprise expressed, and they were proceeding to seriously discuss the master's astonishing conduct when Mr. Spurgeon's gravity began to give way, and it was soon recollected by several that Mrs. Charlesworth had recently presented her husband with a son.

A member of the Tabernacle asked him to call and see her daughter, who said she was ill and could not get up. The mother did not believe there was anything really the matter, except that she had got into a desponding frame of mind, and would make herself believe she was ill. Mr. Spurgeon went to see the young woman, and judged the case to be as the mother had told him. He said to the girl,

'Come, you must get up; your mother believes, and I believe, there is nothing really the matter with you; but if you persist in thinking you are ill you may lie here and die. But remember God has got His own place to which He sends suicides.' The girl seemed startled, and said, 'I will come to the Tabernacle on Sunday.' She did so, and gave her mother no further trouble. Many doubtless see the divine when they most need the physician, but others seek the physician when they most need the divine.

A Church praised the preaching of a student, but offered him only £50 per year as salary. Mr. Spurgeon said they gave him plenty of praise, but offered him precious little pudding. To a deacon he once said, 'You give your pastor mighty poor pay.' 'Well, sir, we get mighty poor preaching.'

Speaking of Monte Carlo, he said it was as fair a spot as there was in all creation, but on account of its gambling he could not think of it as anything else than 'the Devil's marine residence.'

When he first sought membership with a Christian Church the minister, having heard he was a rather high Calvinist, said to him, 'Do you believe it obligatory in Christians to observe the moral law?' The youthful applicant looked at him with astonishment and replied, 'Whose umbrella have I stolen?'

He told us in college of one rather pompous but ignorant local preacher saying, 'I don't see what a man wants to go to college for to learn about *Plateo* and *Kichero* afore he can preach; reading the Bible is enough for me.'

He bade us one Conference to try and find excuses for any weakness in our deacons or Church members, and told us of one undoubtedly good man who every now and again was overcome by fits of temper. It was a mystery to all who knew him, for he was usually most gracious and devout. When he died a surgeon examined his head, and found a little bit of bone protruding into the brain. The mystery of his occasional irritability was thereby explained. 'But, gentlemen,' added the President, 'if you ever get into a temper don't excuse yourselves by thinking a bit of bone is sticking into your brain.'

In introducing a certain diminutive speaker to an audience, he said, 'He is like the cabman's horse, not much to look at, but a good 'un to go.'

I believe I have Scriptural warrant for riding in a carriage. One Baptist minister, as we read in the Acts, rode in one once. It is never recorded that a Presbyterian did.

I don't like dancing. It was through a dance that the first Baptist minister lost his head, and I may well be afraid of it.

With some to whom we preach, the Word does indeed have 'free course,' for it goes in one ear and out at the other.

You cannot measure fire by the bushel, nor prayers by their length.

I preached once at a church where desolation had for a long time reigned. After the service two of the deacons, propping up a wall with their backs and with their hands in their pockets, essayed to speak to me. I said, 'I suppose you are the two pillars of this church.' They were proud to acknowledge it was even so. I saw at once the explanation of non-success.

Don't preach too long. I should say, if you are earnest and interesting, that, whatever you are preaching about, you should preach about forty minutes. Some sermons remind me of the sailor who was told to pull a rope on board; he pulled, and pulled, until he was tired, and then declared that he believed 'the end of this 'ere rope is cut off.'

I was with him when a Scotch lady was praising up the Scotch metrical version of the Psalms. 'Some of them are very good, doubtless, but not all,' said he. Then with a twinkle in his eye, as though bent on a tease, he offered a specimen:

> 'Happy the man, thrice happy he,
> Who, riding on his knaggy,
> He takes the bairns upon his knee,
> And dash them 'gainst the craggy.'

The following are some of the things which he said when lecturing to the students:

The men with pigeon-chests go soonest to heaven. If any of you have tendencies that way, seek expansion by any and every lawful means.

Spiritual life depends on the purposes we cherish.

Pray so much, brethren, that the watching angels shall say, 'These ministers are always coming.'

Prayer meetings are the throbbing machinery of the Church.

There are dungeons underneath the Castle of Despair as dreary as the abodes of the lost; and some of us have been in them.

To learn to say 'No' will be of far greater service than to know Latin.

Stick to your preaching, and let nothing take you from it. If you have not finished your sermon, and should hear the sound of the archangel's trump, go on with it.

Don't be so absorbed, like some brethren, with the doctrine of the Second Coming that you neglect to preach the first. I should like to say to some I know, 'Ye men of Plymouth, why stand ye gazing up into heaven? Go on with your work.'

We are to feed men with the bread of life; but this does not mean we are to ram a quartern loaf down their throats.

The cross of Christ is but dimly seen in Jeremy Taylor's works. He has too much of the art of man, and too little of the heart of God.

Some seem to believe in a new birth once a week. A Methodist once said to me, 'See this man coming down the street? Now he has been born again five times. It is no use his being converted unless he is a teetotaller.' But the Bible knows nothing of such doctrine. Christians are born again once, but never again and again. We believe in *re*-generation, but not in *re-re*-regeneration.

All joy is gone from our life if substitution be untrue.

King Saul was within an inch of glory, and might have had a

dynasty for ever.

Nothing less than to see men new creatures in Christ Jesus must satisfy us. Many will utterly slay drunkenness, and hang a bit of blue ribbon over its grave, yet all the while remain utterly bad at heart.

The lives of many deform the commandments rather than perform them. The bulk of professors, God have mercy on them!

If I do not respond to the appeals of all you ministers for help, don't blame me. You often make my pocket to be the ideal of immutability, for it can say, 'There is no change in me.'

Some people seem to me to have three hands: a right hand, a left hand, and a little behind hand.

Be punctual. Some men won't be in time in eternity. As for myself, I never mean to be the *late* Mr. Spurgeon as long as I live.

The Plymouth Brethren reject our idea of the ministry. Yet many of them have been like the Irishman who went to school and said of it, 'None of us know'd nothin', and we each larn'd one another.'

Mind you are always consistent with yourselves. Yet not like the woman who, when in court, was asked by the judge, 'How old are you?' replied, 'Thirty.' 'Why, I heard you give the same age three years ago.' 'Yes, yer honour, but I am not one of those people who say one thing today, and another tomorrow.'

Some people with a little success in Christian work are like the boy who has caught a tiny fish and cries, 'Jack, look 'ere, Jack, I've got a big 'un.'

A man all jokes is like a dish of beef all horse-radish.

Many business men know nothing about the world except that it is round like an orange, and that it is their duty to squeeze as much of the juice out of it as they can get.

I was stepping out of France into Italy when a Customs officer wanted me to pay duty on some fruit I had with me, but I walked back and ate it.

Those Old Testament men brought great sorrow into their lives by taking more than one wife. They should have first tried living with two tigresses, before trying to be happy with two wives.

Don't give up your work upon every trifling ailment. John Calvin laboured with a complication of forty-nine diseases, yet what a great and grand work he did! John Owen buried ten children, then his wife died, yet he kept on.

If ever you should attempt the grand in your preaching, mind you are sure of not making a fool of yourself, as the brother did who exclaimed, 'It thundered, brethren-it-thundered-like-like-like-anything.' Nor yet as he who, describing the angels ascending and descending Jacob's ladder, said, 'They went up and down, up and down, like-like-' But he did not know what to liken their movements to, but only made himself look like a fool. If you attempt the tight-rope, be sure you are a Blondin first, or you may come a cropper.

Lot was a sorry Lot indeed. Yet his wife was his worse half.

A man who is great on prophecy wrote to me saying he could make the name of Gladstone and of Napoleon and of others tally with the numbers of the beast in the Revelation, but could not make mine, and wanted me to tell him if I knew why. 'I suppose it's because I am not a beast,' was my reply.

The Bible never tells us to get out of debt; it tells us we are not to have any.

I regard a debt on a place of worship as a bad social example.

Society is a contrivance to enable a lot of people to keep each other in countenance.

Avoid carelessness in every part of your work. A clergyman in conducting the Burial Service over a person came to 'this our beloved -' But he did not know if he was burying man or woman, and turned to one of the mourners with the question, 'Brother or sister?' 'Neither, sir, only a friend,' was the bewildering reply.

The buildings in which you will preach were erected as monuments to the power of the doctrines of grace. Mind you preach these doctrines in them. The doctrines some now preach could not build a mouse-trap.

If you bawl much in your preaching, you will soon bawl yourself into glory.

The ten tribes of Israel are not lost. The Jews of today are made up of all the tribes.

Jeremy Taylor is the prince of all Church writers, the poet of the pulpit. But he is too flowery. You must not wrap garlands round your sword if you want to deal effectively with sinners.

Yes, deal with men about their souls whenever you get a suitable opportunity. But mind the opportunity is suitable. I was crossing the Channel one day with my friend Mr. --, who was suffering terribly from seasickness. An over-zealous evangelist was on board, who persisted in speaking to my friend about his soul. 'How long is it since you said you found the Lord, brother?' 'Yah!' said my friend over the side of the boat.

If thy brother smite thee on the one cheek, turn to him the other also. If he hits that, then another law comes in, that of self-preservation, and you should either go from him or go for him.

The Incarnation is the most stupendous miracle of all the ages.

Seneca said, 'No man sets a better rate upon virtue than he that loseth a good name to keep a good conscience.' Let us be willing to do that.

Plead with your young people to make friends early with God and spend a lifetime in His company.

The religion of Jesus puts no restraint upon innocent and healthy pleasure.

If you preach so as to convert souls, the Lord will not disappoint you.

In the ministry to keep on keeping on you will find your chief difficulty.

I observed the other day a marine store notice, 'Fifty tons of bones wanted.' Yes, I thought, and mostly backbones.

It is the glory of Omnipotence to work by improbabilities.

We must make the Church a school to educate the conscience. Many a man has enough conscience to scare him in sin, but not enough to save him from sin.

Cardiphonia is the language of the heart; let your sermons be full of it.

Don't be squeamish in the pulpit, like one who read, 'Jonah was three days and three nights in - ahem - the society of the fish'

Always in your preaching act upon the principle of the military gentleman who ordered his men to fire a salute. 'We've no more ammunition,' said the men. 'Then cease firing.' Gentlemen, stop when your ammunition's done.

I owe more to variety than to profundity in my preaching.

More flies are caught with honey than with vinegar. Preach much on the love of God.

Some people seem to have found a text which says, 'Groan in the Lord always, and again I say, Groan.'

'Lead me not into temptation' means, to me, Bring me not into a committee.

How to balance charity with truth and brotherliness with honesty are in these days intricate questions.

A member once said to his minister who wanted a little more salary as his family increased, 'I did not know you preached for money.' 'No, I don't,' said the minister. 'I thought you preached for souls.' 'So I do; but my family cannot live on souls, and if they could it would take a good many of the size of yours to make a meal.'

The common places of the Bible are the green pastures of truth. Don't be afraid to lead your people into them.

Don't expect to please some people. John came neither eating nor drinking - he was a Good Templar - but they said, He hath a devil. Jesus came eating and drinking, but that did not suit. Live to please God.

Cowper's spirit was broken in his boyhood, which may account somewhat for the melancholy from which he suffered in his manhood. Give your children a blithesome training. You should get Cowper's Letters and read them.

Faith in God produces a higher life and greater gratitude than any other principle. They live indeed who live by faith.

Every lack of veracity indicates some latent vice.

Do your utmost to preserve peace in the Church. Some men seem to think God ordained them to be celestial hedgehogs or spiritual porcupines. Such regard a row as a means of grace.

That which cost thought is likely to excite thought.

In some men God seems to have to create a capacity and moral sense before He can convert them.

Great saints have generally had great natures.

The essence of faith lies in the heart's choice of Christ.

The best way to honour a faithful man is to be like him.

Don't grumble at your Church officers. Believe God gave you these tools to work with; and if they are not exactly to your mind, prove your greatness by doing great work with poor tools.

Characters that are really great are always simple.

Brethren, why don't you come up to the front? *You will always find plenty of room at the front.*

Perfect men generally beat their wives, or do some other useful service for society.

It is as much a difficulty to rejoice evermore as to pray without ceasing.

I like to go into the pulpit saying, 'God be merciful to me a sinner.'

Some reputed as men of genius have only the genius of the monkey, which consists in tearing everything to pieces, the Word of God included. *Geniasses*, I call them.

Feed the poor, as well as preach to them. The hearts of men are often reached through their stomachs.

Don't be afraid to ask neighbouring ministers to come and help you. Say to other Churches as one drover did to another, 'Bill, lend me a bark of your dog.'

It is a great mercy to be a minister. Preaching has often driven me to my knees and chained me to my Bible.

Paul hung up his selfishness by the neck. Mind you do the same.

I like to lie and soak in my text.

We ought to be careful in street preaching not to annoy the residents. One man offered an open-air preacher to be converted if he would only go.

We must educate the Church to confirm the witness of the Gospel.

Ritualism is an expression of the innate idolatry of the human heart. It can only be distinguished from Romanism by Omniscience. They shall yet be buried in the same family grave.

If you are true to God, what lives yours will be! - borne along on the wings of Providence until you shall exchange them for the wings of angels.

Let the love of Christ be the controlling element of your life.

Christ crucified will be the library which triumphant souls will study to all eternity.

Sinners pass a brief career of blindness, then go down into deeper darkness.

Make Christ the diamond setting of every sermon.

Always insist on the congregations coming to the prayer meeting.

One great object of Church teaching should be to educate efficient workers 'unto the work of ministering'.

The sisterhood is one of the most powerful agencies in the Church of Rome. So it should be with us.

Matthew Henry says, 'If religion has done nothing for your tempers, it has done nothing for your souls.'

Self is the only oil which makes the chariot wheels of the hypocrite move in religious concern.

If the Devil were to sift some professors through a hair-sieve, he would not find any religion in them.

Learn to love the burdens Christ gives you to bear.

The life of a Christian should be the best picture of Christ.

The life of Christ was so holy that if He had been a mere man He deserved to be God.

A good life will no more conduce to a sinner's justification than will a wicked one.

God ever connects special success with a special state of heart.

Christ's presence with you in the service will fill it with more than the fragrance of a thousand flowers.

There is a distinct connection between importunate, agonising prayer and true success.

Ghosts cannot stand the light, nor devils love.

Be sure you read Thomas Adams, and Sibbes, and Isaac Ambrose. Get Robert Bowden, too; he is a master of experience.

Southey's *Commonplace Book* will well pay for reading.

People are generally lean that lean towards Arminianism.

Dean Swift said in his day, 'There is most religion among the middle classes: the top is all froth, the bottom all dregs.' I am afraid it is so today.

Condensed thought in books is what we want. We can boil it down afterwards, and make soup of it.

The grace of God will teach you to be exact and circumspect in little things. I believe it will teach a lad to play marbles without cheating.

If you preach what is new, it won't be true. If you preach what is true, it won't be new.

In the night of sorrow sinners are like owls, believers like nightingales, and they sing in the darkness. There is no real night to a man of a nightingale spirit.

Gardening is the only occupation which is not the effect of sin. When Adam was as yet unfallen God put him in the garden to keep and dress it.

Beseech Christ to chisel His likeness into your features somehow.

Be willing, if necessary, to live in a spirit of perpetual martyrdom for Christ. Paul was.

If in speaking you fish for claps, you will deserve a clap behind.

I have seen husbands obeying their wives, but I have never much admired the conduct

It is terrible to think that the lapsed masses have been in our Sunday schools.

We must get at artisans by artisans.

There could have been no moral government without permission to sin.

A real heart is the main qualification for a great soulwinner.

Appeal not so much to men's fears as to their sense of right.

In a single verse old Dr. Watts has admirably taught the art of prayer. I will give it to you.

> Call upon God, adore, confess,
> Petition, plead, and then declare
> You are the Lord's. Give thanks and bless,
> And let Amen conclude the prayer.

Meekness consists in taking meekly offences against yourself, not in being careless about sins against God.

'From henceforth thou shalt catch men.' Only *He* can make us man-catchers.

These fishermen were as the briar on which He could graft the rose of *His* grace.

To win sinners we must be men of ardent religious affections.

Character is the great secret of religious eloquence.

The best relief from sorrow is to sing.

Mercy is God's Benjamin, the last born and best beloved of His attributes; He delighteth in mercy.

Elijah prayed that he might die, yet he never was to die, and never did. Often thank God for not answering many of your prayers.

Every man sees God according to his own condition.

If I am a lost child of God, He will be a bigger loser than I am. I only lose myself, but He loses His honour, His name, His glory.

Arvine's *Anecdotes* will be of great service to you. But he was an awful teetotaller. He almost makes you believe that the smell of a gin bottle washed out sixteen years before has ruined souls.

Some men are grand trenchers, though they are poor in the trenches.

Some preachers have no settled doctrine. When I was at Pompeii I saw a goldsmith shop. He had several statues finished up to the face; the faces of these were in the adjoining room, to suit purchasers. Some preachers' doctrines are made to order.

I believe in a committee of three, myself to be the lecting constituency; one of the committee to be always away, and the other in bed.

Jesus did not commit Himself unto men, because He knew what

was in them; how much less should we, because we don't know what is in them!

Men who conquer go in for attack.

Never have a meeting you cannot invite Christ to.

For improvement in style read the *Letters of Junius*, published by Woodfall.

The following points of an address to the students may be helpful to many. He gave it under the title of 'Short Precepts, or Securities of Success.'

1. Be sure you are called.

2. Go in for a high ideal.
Set before you something apostolic - Baxter, Bunyan, Whitefield. Have an ideal, and intend to reach it.

3. Make yourselves qualified for the best possible positions. To do this, you must continue to grow when you leave college.

4. Especially seek spiritual attainments.
Be sure you are men of humility, prayer, faith, and of love for God and souls.

5. Overcome all mental and moral defects.
Master your temper. Don't be sombre, don't be too light.
Mental defects. - Be careful of mental squints; let the eyes of your mind look right on. Be logical, be accurate, be clear in your thinking as a crystal stream.

6. Study the most successful models.

There is much in this. I made Whitefield my model years ago. Buy his sermons, published by Milner and Sowerby. There are volumes of his sermons which do not faithfully represent him.

7. Try every available method.

With the people, with yourselves, hard study, days of prayer.

8. Be humbly willing to be corrected.

9. Be sure you feel what you preach, and preach what you feel. Get a red-hot heart, and preach to the heart.

10. Give sound matter, and plenty of it.

11. Put up with anything, even with cross-grained deacons and poverty.

12. Subject every desire in your soul to the one object of life; be willing to forego high scholarship, or getting married, if these would hinder you in soul winning.

13. Seek grace to be always intense.

14. Ask Divine guidance about every little thing.

15. Be a pastor, be a saint, be an intercessor, be a martyr if necessary, and success surely awaits you.

The following are brief notes of an address to the students on *points not to be forgotten.*

1. Every man must be a consecrated man.

It is only to consecrated men we wish to give training. Remember that always in work, in recreation, and in all domestic relationships you are consecrated men. Where ever you are, whatever you are doing, never forget that the sacred crimson is upon you.

2. Now you are consecrated you must lay yourselves out to serve God. In college you are to serve Him by the acquisition of knowledge. God will appoint you other work tomorrow, but today's duty is the duty of today.

3. Remember that opportunities for usefulness are yours today which will never come again. You have, as students, advantages which once gone will be gone for ever.

4. Nothing will come out of you that is not in you. Only out of fulness of mind and fulness of heart you can give fulness of matter. Seek to gather and retain; then, like the spider with his web, you can spin your sermons out of your own bowels.

5. Every day your character is being formed. You are now clay on the potter's wheel. Yield yourselves utterly to God and to His truth.

6. Cultivate every worthy habit and repress every questionable one. Be punctual. Be particularly clean in yourself, I have seen the nails of some preachers under which you might have grown mustard and cress. Be full of the spirit of perseverance. We have preached our weight of sermons at some men without apparently any spiritual

results. In one of the battles between the French and Germans it is said that 6,000 shots were fired for every man killed. So often in preaching we must take better aim. Many sinners seem bullet-proof, but we must get at them somehow. Go to their houses and dine with them, and get familiar with their joints.

Vary the tone of your voice often; be like the weather, have sun, sleet, rain, then dry up, anything but fog: don't mystify the Gospel, nor yet parsonify it.

At different times Mr. Spurgeon's talks to the students took the form of a sermon. I have many of the outlines of these. Some of them have been published, as he afterwards delivered them in the Tabernacle, although I can find no record of many others in any of his works. I will give two brief sketches of these sermonic lectures.

JUDGES XVI. 6
'Tell me, I pray thee, wherein thy great strength lieth.'

I. The believer is a man of great strength.
   He masters lions of temptation and affliction.
   He removes posts of difficulty.
   He snaps the bonds of evil habits.
   He conquers all sorts of foes.

II. His strength is a secret.
   It does not lie where the strength of others lies, in education, wealth, honour, the bank; nor yet where many a woman's strength does - in her tongue.
   It lies in God.
   In prayer.
   In faith.
   In consecration.

III. Enemies seek to deprive him of this strength.

IV. He should guard it well, lest he be deprived of it.
If he lose it he will be as weak as others.
He will lose his eyes.
Be in prison.
Have to grind.
He will make Israel mourn, and the Philistines glad.

The delivery of the above was a solemn, heart-searching occasion. Many a student then present can never forget what he felt. It has proved one of the safeguards of life to not a few.

The following sermon was of a very different sort, but in its way equally helpful.

PSALM CXIX. 30, 3 I, 32

'I have chosen the way of truth: Thy judgments have I laid before me. I have stuck unto Thy testimonies: O Lord, put me not to shame. I will run the way of Thy commandments, when Thou shalt enlarge my heart.'

Here we have chosen, stuck, run. Choice, perseverance, progress. Make a good choice, or you won't stick.

I. The choice. The way of truth.
1. I did this experimentally when the Holy Spirit showed me the way of lies. Then I chose Christ - the way of truth.

2. I have done this doctrinally.
   I saw what was the mind of the Spirit, the most Scriptural

form of belief, the body of believers walking most nearly to New Testament orders, and I chose the truth, the way of truth.

3. Since we first chose the way of truth we have often done so. False systems have come before us, and may have beguiled us for a little while, but they have utterly disappointed us, and we have chosen the way of truth. Now, if temptation comes like painted harlots to lead us astray, we say, 'It is too late, our mind is made up; I have seen God's way of truth. It may be a hard way, a long way, an unpopular way; but I have chosen it.' 'Thy judgments have I laid before me.' Passion is well, principle is better. I have opened the documents like a lawyer. I have looked into the subjects of Calvinism, free will, and I have made up my mind about them. The longer I live, the more I love my principles. I believe others love them who won't acknowledge it. Arminians get a drop behind the door. They like free grace. Because I have chosen I have laid God's judgments before me, and keep them ever before me. It is a grand thing to get the Word of God into the mind and heart.

11. The choosing man is sticking man.

I have stuck unto Thy testimonies. I am glued, bird-limed to them. I laid hold on them, and they have laid hold on me.

The prayer. 'Put me not to shame.' By making me wise, by keeping me from doing foolish things; put me not to shame. Keep near me, Lord. I have stuck to Thy testimonies, do Thou stick to me.

III. The man who sticks to the testimonies will make progress in God's way.

I am in the right way. Now I will go forward in it with all my might. 'I will run;' this is a warm pace, a healthy pace, a God-honouring pace. Half our joy is in running. Alas! we are so slow, and so our joys are so few. But I will run. I will do much for God. I will be intense, and keep on being intense. All through my ministry this shall be my motto: 'I will run.'

The prayer. 'When Thou shalt enlarge my heart.' When Thou shalt set it free, and make it bigger. We are too often tight! I often get bricked up. But when I get liberty, how I like to run! Wesleys and joy. Make my heart, O God, as big as Solomon's. I want to know more, to believe more, to have large ideas of God, and to run the way of His commandments as swiftly as an eagle flies.

Force and forcibleness in our ministry was the subject of his talk one Friday. The points of which were: First, Our real force is in Divine authority. Secondly, in earnestness of conviction. Thirdly, in concentration. Fourthly, in courage and boldness. Fifthly, specially in our matter. What is said must be clearly said; we must be terse, clear, and to the point. We must use plain words, Saxon words. Using fine, long words and eloquent periods to express your thoughts will be like getting sixteen brewer's horses to draw a perambulator. Mind you don't lose self-possession. Some suffer from abstraction as much as the man who put his watch in the saucepan and looked at the egg to count the minutes.

Sixthly, character and motive will affect the force of our preaching. Be holy and have the single eye, and your ministry must tell. Have confidence in the power of the truth you preach. Don't associate trifles with it. Don't think it necessary to adorn it. Preaching is often weakened by the introduction of the beauties of language. Long words hinder force. Richard Baxter is the most forceful of writers. Read him. Be full of compassion, and let it work into a sacred passion for the glory of God in the salvation of souls.

Looking over my notebooks I find very many of his sayings I have not yet transcribed. I cannot think the reader will weary of them if I give a few more.

Be thankful to God for His mercies, but don't boast of them before men.

Secular employment is consistent with a state of innocency and of deep communion with God, for Adam was a gardener while yet unfallen.

We must never complain of God, but we may complain to Him.

If you ever take two texts for one sermon, mind they are congruous; for example, you must not give out, 'He went and hanged himself' and 'Go thou and do likewise.'

'I will lead on softly' is a good text for a Sunday school sermon.

The first essential for good preaching is the same as for good living, viz. *Faith*; it takes with us the place of demonstration, and sometimes of experience.

Luther trembled before he went into the pulpit, so also did John Welsh and John Newton.

I should like each man to cultivate a high-toned ministry. By tone I don't mean *twang* - avoid that. Plenty of ministers caught McCheyne's twang without his tone of spirit and life.

Let your ministry be high-toned as to its object. Let it be the glory of God. Seek conversions every time you preach. High-toned as to your character. What may be right in others may be wrong in ministers. Be guileless, practise self-denial, cultivate a readiness to forgive. A minister should be willing to be a doorscraper for Christ. High-toned as to your preaching. We are greatly in need of first-class ministers. There are stars against many names in the Handbook.[1] Mind you don't get among the stars. Let your ministry be thorough. Give plenty of good matter. Seek to possess both unction and gumption. Don't go in for a highflown style, it will make you mere play actors. Try to be more holy than McCheyne, more earnest than Baxter. Seek to excel those who excel. To be great you must be good. Then high-toned as to your work for the Lord. The Spartan was first in danger: be brave in your deeds. Really do something for God. Pray much. We ought to pray more than any dozen people in our congregation.

I will give you a short address on *Qualifications for Soul Winning*. The first is *holiness of character*. This is to be seen in communion with God. The force of a sermon ever depends upon what has gone before. Then *spiritual life to a high degree. Also a low opinion of self.* With this man will God dwell. A proud minister delights the devil. Be nothing in the sight of God. Humility is to think rightly of yourself. When Henry V. was very ill he awoke out of his sleep to find his boy Henry VI. trying on his crown. He said, 'Wait a bit, wait until I am dead.' While Jesus lives let the crown be His. The next essential is a *living faith.* In God. In your calling. In your message. Belief in your message will beget faith in it in others. Have faith in power of the message to save. *Thorough earnestness.* The more I think of some men's sermons the less I think of them. *Simplicity of*

---

[1] These are ministers without a charge.

heart and complete surrender of yourself to God. Be to God like a cork on the river to the wave. Be absolutely at His disposal, with no wish to do other than He would have you.

Pay very careful attention to articulation. The majority of young men confound loudness with force. They speak in too high a key.

Here is a good subject for you: 'The children of Israel stripped themselves of their ornaments.' - Exod. xxxiii. 6.

Objections to the doctrines of election. - Calvinism is the highest reason. Even fatalism has been productive of great force and strength of character. But we are not fatalists by any means. Fate is blind. But God is not to us a mere Persian doll, as He seems to be to some people.

A common objection is that of father and children. But this is not to the point at all. Men are guilty. He is King, they His rebellious subjects. They have forfeited all claim. He is at liberty to glorify either His righteousness or His mercy. Israel was the most undeserving of all nations, yet the secret of all their blessing is given in Psalm xliv. 3, thus - 'Because Thou hadst a favour unto them' It is said the doctrine *makes God to be partial.* But cannot He do what He wills with His own? *It makes God arbitrary.* But His will must rule. A God who has no will is no God. Can creatures defeat His purposes? We cannot understand His reason, yet reason is in Him. *It tends to immorality!* But the fact is ignored that men are ordained to sanctification. God is the brave man's hope, but not the coward's excuse. Some hold the doctrine of election; but the doctrine of election never held them, and they are often full of pride and self-esteem. I could say to them what Aristotle once said to a young man, 'I wish I were what you think you are.'

The doctrine is said to *discourage effort, and that it tends to pride.* No! No! Eternal love ever subdues and humbles. And as for discouraging effort, it rather quickens zeal and inspires confidence in the soul. We do not wander among tombs to find if sinners will live of themselves, we take God with us, who has chosen them unto life. Our preaching is like holding a steel magnet.

It is objected *that election implies the decrees of reprobation.* No; God's decrees are unto salvation. Sinners suffer a self-chosen rebellion. Their ruin is from their own door. Yet the two texts in Jude and Peter stand out like two masses of granite to warn men and vindicate God.

Thomas Adams was a divine moralist rather than a theologian. Be sure you get his exposition of 2 Peter. He was the Shakespeare of the pulpit. He says some wonderful things.

It will do you good to read the life of Ignatius, founder of the Jesuits, providing you do so with a saltcellar in front of you. He is a wonderful imitation of the Saviour. The Jesuits sprang up in the Church of Rome and called themselves 'The Society of Jesus.' They are the juice and marrow of Popery. They have done wonders of good. Self was swallowed up in the Society. Each man abandoned himself. Jesuitism is none the less a parody on Jesuism. Ignatius Loyola was born in 1491. He had a duplex character that was most un-understandable. He was the chief opponent of Luther. He went without soles to his boots. I suppose he thought this the best way to save souls. He died at sixty-five, in the year 1556.

Read Bunyan much. His *Holy War* for religious experience. Have the *Pilgrim's Progress* at your finger ends.

Richard Baxter belongs to the end of the great Puritan period. He wrote sixty books, and died at sixty. He did not see that an absolutely fixed predestination is not inconsistent with free agency; but it is not. If you want to know the art of pleading, read him. See especially his sermon on *Making light of it*. Read also his *Reformed Pastor*.

The English owe the great freedom of their constitution to the fidelity of Nonconformists.

A well-trained sisterhood is the noblest of blessings.

Adaptation in preaching. - Those sermons are likely to be blest that were distinctly intended by the preacher to achieve this end. Until God undertakes to ripen wheat by cold, or to illuminate the world by fog, He will never bless some sermons. We must see to it that our sermons are *interesting*. You must tickle the oyster if you want to insert the knife. Let there be plenty of sound *instruction* too. We must have light as well as fire. Some preachers don't know what they are aiming at. Like the boy who, interrupted in his tears, asked, 'What was I crying about?' Truth - truth - truth - give them plenty of it. You must be *impressive* too. Get impressive themes, and cultivate an impressive delivery; some keep to one tone of voice, and that one is not in the scale. Take out of your sermons all that will divert attention; don't be content with less results than conversions. Not as the boy who, when asked if he had caught any fish, said, 'No, but I have drowned a lot of worms.' Be careful of your 'h's.' With many the letter h is the letter that killeth. Sermons fullest of Christ aimed directly at the heart, sermons that have been prayed over, and that are preached in connection with a praying people, these are sure to be blest.

Use your experiences as colours to paint Christ. In preparing a sermon, first choose your subject, then sketch the outline, then collect your materials; then let there be fermentation. (Of course you teetotallers won't do this.)

If you are called upon to preach in the afternoon, be careful what you have for dinner. If you eat half a leg of pork, you won't feel much Divine assistance. A man full of pudding is not very likely to be full of power. The process of digestion won't help your sanctification.

We must ever guard against two foes in preaching-the *pretentious* and the *commonplace.*

Fear, hope, zeal, compassion, love, reverence - these are the harpstrings of nature upon which, as preachers, we have to ever play.

The President gave us the following one Friday; but I am not sure if he read it from some volume he brought with him. 'Three mistakes of Christians. When they look for that in themselves which can only be found in Christ, viz. *Righteousness.* When they look for that in the Law which can only be found in the Gospel, viz. *Mercy.* When they look for that on earth which can only be found in heaven, viz. *Perfection.*' I fancy it is from good old Matthew Henry.

Matthew Henry preached for twenty years on the questions of the Bible.

Trust in Christ is the beam of the morning which marks the beginning of an endless day.

One has said, 'I preached philosophy, and men applauded; I preached the Gospel, and men repented.'

Preach much on the characters of the Bible. The Bible is nearly made up of biography. The parables are studies of character. Some of the characters are very complex; Balaam, for instance. His knowledge was with God, but his will was with riches. He teaches us that a man may be very near an angel and yet a devil, and all the worse devil. We have seen more good in some bad men than in other good ones.

You will do well to read Hooker, Taylor, and Baxter for theology; Bacon, Newton, and Locke for philosophy; and Shakespeare, Spenser, and Milton for poetry.

Learning and the Gospel. - Learning is not absolutely necessary for success in the ministry. It is a fact that many have been instrumental in soul winning who have not had learning. The power of learning has often worked against the Gospel. There is no necessary relationship between the two. I have seen learning stand in opposition to the conversion of sinners. There is a learning that is essential to a successful ministry, viz. the learning of the whole Bible, to know God by prayer, and by experience of His dealings. Always treasure up your experience. Yet I would have you go in for learning to the utmost. If you seek increase of grace as well as increase of knowledge, learning can only be a blessing. It will develop your powers of mind, enlarge your experience, and help you to understand the Scriptures. Only don't trust in your education; that won't save souls. Never glory in learning, and don't look down on a brother who has not got it, and don't neglect other duties to obtain it.

There are no illustrations so good as those from Scripture.

There are many excellent texts in Hosea.

Everybody was against Jeremiah, yet they would not go to Egypt without him.

The way to be ever wise in action is to live in close communion with Christ.

A minister who is a mere man-pleaser is a soul destroyer. We should study to draw groans from sinners, rather than applause. One soul won to Christ is better than a thousand merely moralised and still sleeping in their sins.

Frequently visit your Sabbath schools, if it is only to walk through them.

Have the Holy Ghost in your hearts, your minds developed, and your bodies in subjection, and success is sure.

Virtuous self-government is not only right in itself, but it improves the inward constitution of our characters.

Improvement can only come to you by constant effort.

The footsteps of misery always follow self-neglect.

A faithful minister is sure to be respected. See how Herod respected John.

Don't lament over your poverty. The men who bless the world most are not the rich men. Intellectual wealth is far better than any other. Many ministers are troubled about the future of their children; yet ministers' sons and daughters do as well as those of tradesmen and merchants. Even a poor minister may influence others to pour streams of wealth into the treasury of Christ.

Always have one hymn of praise in the service.

Don't put your best Sunday clothes on to pray, or they won't know you at the Gate of Mercy.

Preach nothing down but the devil, and nothing up but Christ.

Your mouth will be a flowing stream or a sealed fountain, according as your heart is.

The more success you meet with, the more difficulties you will meet with too. But mind you don't create needless difficulties. 'What a deal we have to suffer in the service of God!' said the monk, when he burned his finger with a hot chicken.

There is something very holy in a true man's tears.

Calvinism presents less difficulty than any rival system.

The Epistle to the Romans is the loftiest piece of writing in the human tongue.

The tears of affliction are often needed to keep the eye of faith bright.

There is honey in every cup of affliction which God puts into the hand of the Christian; but generally he has to wait until he reaches the bottom before he can taste it.

A poet has said:

> I've heard of hearts unkind, kind deeds
> With coldness still returning;
> Alas! the gratitude of men
> Hath oftener left me mourning.

But the gratitude of men never left me mourning.

When God wants to water my garden, He sends a shower all over Clapham, and yet it is for my garden He does it. This is how Christians view their mercies. 'Who loved *me*, and gave Himself for *me*.'

The above are samples of his college talk. They might be further extended. I find I have notes of his lectures on 'A Well-balanced Ministry,' 'The Use of the Emotions in Preaching,' 'Poverty in the Ministry,' and on 'Style.' His lectures delivered during later years were generally, though not invariably, taken down in shorthand by his private secretary, Mr. Harrald. But the earlier ones were not often reported, and many of them were never repeated. Those who heard them count it no mean loss that they cannot be fully recovered or recalled.

It has been my good fortune to preserve not only many of the gems of his speech given in college, but to retain and obtain not a few of his utterances upon different occasions outside the college walls. Some of these may prove a fitting conclusion to this chapter of table talk.

Speaking at the stone-laying of a Baptist chapel, he said: 'I do not approve of stone-laying ceremonies, and believe them to be often a waste of time; that money can be had as well without them.

'This is to be a Baptist chapel. I am not ashamed of the name, nor afraid of being called sectarian. Some folks cannot belong to any Church, for fear of being called sectarian, though it generally happens that these people are the most sectarian of all - forming a new sect, which might well be named the Me-ites.'

Concerning marriage ceremonies he said: 'For my own part I hope the time may come when marriages in a place of worship will be done away with altogether; when marriages in every case will be but a civil agreement, and then afterwards a religious service in whatever place may be chosen.'

Education without religion is like the solar system without the sun.

If the Sabbath joint is only a grim scraggy bit of mutton with plenty of divisions and nothing to divide, you will soon discover that your people will not be satisfied.

Our preaching is to many people much like a fiddler's play; they come to see how we do it. But I don't care what they think of me, so long as they are blessed by what I say.

He said to his people once that he could only tell them over again that he believed he had been a piece of cotton stretched across sugar, and people had crystallised round him. Why, they being the sugar, and he the cotton, they had crystallised round him he could not tell.

Almost any fool can go first, but it takes an uncommonly wise man to go second.

I always go in for raising everybody's wages, my own included.

The worst harm that uncharitable brethren can do us is to render us as uncharitable as themselves.

Instead of finding fault with your brother you should think, 'What is that to me?' You must correct the mistakes of others certainly; but if you see a crooked stick in the Lord's bundle, be perfectly straight yourself, and getting alongside the crooked one, loving friendship will do the rest.

We must stoop before God that we may conquer amongst men.

Many people have a very neat little Bible and a very big ledger; the Bible gets buried under the ledger.

He who rules the waves, rules the waves of human thought as well as the waves of the sea.

When I cannot understand anything in the Bible, it seems to me as though God had set a chair there for me, at which to kneel and worship; and that the mysteries are intended to be an altar of devotion.

It is God's Word which does the work of saving souls and of elevating the Church. Instead of the wooden swords of modern thought let us take the good old Jerusalem blade.

Sins are called 'wild oats,' but they will have an awful reaping.

He said he was once speaking to a gentleman who said: 'Well, I am not a Christian, I am what is called an Agnostic' He said, "That is Greek, is it not?' The gentleman replied that it was. Whereupon he rejoined, 'Well, that word in Latin is " ignoramus."'

Speaking to policemen he said: Some of you cannot travel very fast to heaven because there are so many bars on the road.

I wonder which is the worse - the man who can preach and will not, or the man who cannot preach, but will.

Some ministers do not believe the Lord is with their Gospel, and they have to catch men by such pretences as can be devised, like the servant who caught and killed flies on purpose to stick them on to fly paper.

At the last Conference he attended he said: I believe the Second Coming of Christ will be soon, judging by signs. The devil is very busy, and when you see a farmer burning gates and destroying the barns, you may be sure his lease is up.

Some ministers have a shell, and crawl into it just before they begin to preach.

There are some brethren who are like large barrels, but they put the tap at the top, and very little comes out. Put the tap at the bottom, brethren.

How many prayers are like the grocer's bills, 'Ditto, ditto, ditto,' or 'As per usual.'

Give up the Bible? We would sooner give up our lives. Doubt the inspiration of the Bible? Some of us never can, for it has inspired us; and when a book inspires a man, he knows the book itself must be inspired.

Harvesting is sometimes hard work, but it is always pleasant. No harvestman can carry on his work throughout the entire year, but he is glad when harvest time comes. So in the Church.

Some trees that grow slowly are most magnificent ones when they have grown.

They say in Mentone that if there is a room into which the sun does not enter, the physician must.

A dog used to come through a broken fence in my garden, doing gardening that I did not like. One day I flung a stick at him. The creature seized the stick and laid it at my feet. That dog beat me by trusting. I patted him on the head and said, 'Good dog; come as often as you like.' Faith will bring even God's thunderbolts and lay them at His feet.

I like to see a man trying to do the impossible. Any fool can do what he can do.

When a youth I said, 'I think I am bound to give myself unto reading, and not to grieve the Spirit by unthought-of effusions.'

The expending of money on mere show at funerals is absurd, unthrifty, and even cruel ...To bedeck a corpse in vain trappings is a grim unsuitability.

King Jesus looks upon the death of His saints as the last struggle of their life conflict.

Every man must serve somebody: we have no choice as to that fact. Those who have no master are slaves to themselves.

I am usually careless of the notices of papers concerning myself - referring all honours to my Master, and believing that dishonourable articles are but advertisements for me, and bring people under the sound of the Gospel.

We mistake our divergences of judgment for differences of heart, but they are far from being the same thing. In these days of infidel criticism, believers of all sorts are driven together. For my part, I believe that all spiritual persons are already one. (*Sword and Trowel.*)

If you question God, He will soon leave you to question yourselves.

A home should be a Bethel, not a Babel … If I had no home, the world would be like a big prison to me.

'Jesus!' 'Tis a pearl dissolved, 'tis a sonnet rolled into a word, 'tis a great oratorio in five letters, 'tis the essence of music condensed into two syllables.

Don't go creeping into your subject, first to the ankles and then to the knees, as some preachers do, but plunge into it at once over head and ears; that is the way to get the attention of the people. Don't spar at them, but hit out boldly, straight from the shoulder.

Of a popular orator he said: He pays out sovereigns occasionally, but he has no fourpenny bits for ordinary use.

Hammer away with the old Gospel, and let those who like it use the miserable wooden mallet of mere reason.

Brother Pierson, I am a very wilful man. If people don't do as I want them, they are generally very sorry for it afterwards.

When some one asked him once, 'Who can possibly take your place when you are gone?' he replied, 'I never trouble myself as to who shall marry my wife after I am dead.'

I dare say our fathers were poor weavers, but I had far rather be descended from one who has suffered for the faith than bear the blood of all the emperors within my veins.

A Pharisee may polish up into an ordinary Christian; but somehow there is a charming touch about the pardoned sinner which is lacking in the other.

I am not quite sure about a smile being a sin, and at any rate I think it less a crime to cause momentary laughter than a half-hour's slumber.

Little sins are like little thieves, they open the door to big ones.

I will respect you, whatever your theological views. Only stand to your guns.

If a man should come to me and say, 'Mr. Spurgeon, may I go to the theatre?' I should reply, 'Do you want to go to the theatre? If so, you must go, and take it as an evidence that you need grace in your heart.'

When books fail me I offer this prayer: 'O Lord, teach me what this means;' and it is marvellous how a hard flinty text strikes out sparks with the steel of prayer.

Parliamentary government seems to me to be becoming rapidly impossible. It is all jaw and no work nowadays.

The following was given in the *Pall Mall Gazette* a few years ago:

Three young fellows came into the Tabernacle, and settled

themselves conspicuously in the gallery with their hats on. In vain the officials requested them to uncover. Of course Mr. Spurgeon's eye was soon on them, and, leading his discourse round to the respect which all Christians are bound to show for the feelings of others, he said, 'My friends, the other day I went into a Jewish synagogue, and I naturally uncovered my head, but on looking round I perceived that all the rest wore their hats, and so, not wishing to offend against what I supposed to be their reverent practice, though contrary to my own, I conformed to the Jewish use and put on my hat. I will now ask those three young Jews up in the gallery to show the same deference to our Christian practice in the House of God as I was prepared to show them when I visited their synagogue, and take off their hats.'

I hate oratory. I come down as low as I can. Highflying and fine language seems to me wicked when souls are perishing.

During the baptismal regeneration controversy he once met a minister who said to him, 'I hear, friend Spurgeon, that you are in hot water.' 'Oh dear no,' said Mr. Spurgeon, 'I am not in hot water; the other fellows are. I am the man who makes the water boil.'

At a tea meeting he was discussing the benefactions which a well-known person had bestowed on various charities. 'Do you know,' said he, 'that man's fortune has been swollen by dancing saloons to which are attached private apartments? If such a man does not go to the devil, I don't see what use it is to have a devil at all.'

Dr. Wood, an American, while in London, was telling Mr. Spurgeon that he was going to Germany to study. 'Haven't you any theological seminaries in America?' asked Mr. Spurgeon. 'Yes,' said Dr. Wood; 'but I don't think I know everything, though I graduated at Princeton and I am going to Germany to try and learn more.' 'Well,' said Mr. Spurgeon, 'I hope you will not be like the calf I once heard of. The milk of one cow was not enough for it, so they gave it the milk of two, and the more milk it drank the more of a calf it became.'

When Mr. Spurgeon first came to London Mr. Aldis was pastor of Maze Pond Church. One evening several Baptist ministers of the South of London met together for tea and mutual conference. At the close they knelt together for prayer. One of my predecessors in the ministry prayed for Mr. Spurgeon thus: 'O Lord, bless Thy young servant before Thee, who has so much to learn and so much to unlearn.' Mr. Aldis afterwards expressed himself unfavourably as to the manner in which the prayer was offered, and said, 'Mind how you treat that young man, for if I am not greatly mistaken he will yet be one of the greatest preachers of this age - he has a fervour of spirit, a command of language, and an imagination such as I never knew in one so young.'

The late Paxton Hood said of him, 'His humility kills me; I feel I am no Christian at all when I am with Spurgeon.'

He once wrote in the album of a friend, 'I would rather be a minister than an emperor. I would rather preach the Gospel than I would fly like an angel.'

In the midst of a circle of friends he spoke of a big offer of money he had received to lecture, but which he had declined, and then added, 'Nobody will know until I am dead how little C. H. Spurgeon cared for money.'

He described a Pharisee as having his halfpenny in one hand ready for the collection, and a trumpet in the other ready to call attention to his generosity.

Speaking at Mr. Booth's blue-ribbon army meeting he said: A horse cannot say Yea, but he can say Neigh.

There are three kinds of people in the world: the wills, the won'ts, and the can'ts. The first accomplish everything; the second oppose everything; the third fail in everything.

That fellow is just like a telescope. You can draw him out, see through him, and shut him up again.

I never like people to tell me secrets, for I cannot keep them.

We notice frequently over cemetery gates, as an emblematic device, a torch turned over, ready to be quenched. Ah, my brethren, it is not so; the torch of our life burns the better and blazes the brighter for the change of death. The breaking of the pitcher shall be so remodelled as to become an aid to that light; its present breaking is but preparatory to its future refashioning.

CHAPTER VII

HIS CHOICE CORRESPONDENCE

SEVERAL of Mr. Spurgeon's letters have already been given in preceding pages; but a brief chapter dealing with his letter-writing may not be out of place. Of them we may say:

They live, they speak, they breathe what love inspires,
Warm from the soul, and faithful to its fires.

He was so circumstanced that from his first advent in London his correspondence was very large, and it reached ultimately to enormous proportions. 'I am immersed to the chin in letters,' was his own indication once to me of what his letter-writing entailed. I know one gentleman who possesses eighty epistles from him, and I heard of another who counts among his chief treasures quite a large number received from him during a period extending over many years. I am the happy possessor of not a few. But, knowing as I did the labour and time his correspondence cost him, I refrained as much as possible from adding to his task. Moreover, as I was privileged so frequently to see him, there was not the necessity in my case for very frequent communication by post. But there must be in existence in England, America, the Colonies, and other parts of the world, where Christian English speaking people are to be found, many hundreds, if not many thousands, of letters and postcards written with his own hand.

Of those written prior to his settlement in London we quote only one. In his fifteenth year Mr. Spurgeon wrote the following letter to his uncle, in which, as George Needham says, 'The vigour of his mind, the boldness of his faith, and the strength of his will, are clearly manifest.'

My DEAR UNCLE, - Dumb men make no mischief. Your silence and my neglect make one think of the days when letters were costly and not of penny postage. You have doubtless heard of me as a top-tree Antinomian. I trust you know enough of me to disbelieve it. It is an object of my life to disprove the slander. I groan daily under a body of sin and corruption. Oh, for the time when I shall drop this flesh and be free from sin! I become more and more convinced that to attempt to be saved by a mixed covenant of works and faith is, in the words of Berridge, 'to yoke a snail with an elephant.' I desire to press forward for direction to my Master in all things; but as to trusting to my own obedience or righteousness, I should be worse than a fool and ten times worse than a madman. Poor dependent creatures! prayer had need be our constant employment; the foot of the throne our continual dwelling-place; for the Rock of Ages is our only safe Hiding-place.

I rejoice in an assured knowledge by faith of my interest in Christ, and of the certainty of my eternal salvation. Yet what strivings, what conflicts, what dangers, what enemies stand in my way! The foes in my heart are so strong, that they would have killed me and sent me to hell long ere this, had the Lord left me; but, blessed be His name!

His electing, redeeming, and saving love has got fast hold of me; and who is able to pluck me out of my Father's hand? On my bended knees I have often to cry for succour; and, bless His name! He has hitherto heard my cry. Oh, if I did not know that all the Lord's people had soul-contention, I should give up all for lost! I rejoice that the promises left on record are meant for me as well as for every saint of His, and as such I desire to grasp them. Let the whole earth, and even God's professing people, cast out my name as evil; my Lord and Master, He will not. I glory in the distinguishing grace of God, and will not, by the grace of God, step one inch from my principles, or think of adhering to the present fashionable sort of religion. Oh, could I become like holy men of past ages - fearless of men - holding sweet communion with God - weaned more from the world, and enabled to fix my thoughts on spiritual things entirely! But when I would serve God, I find my old deceitful heart, full of the very essence of hell, rising up into my mouth, polluting all I say and do.

What should I do if, like you, I were called to be engaged about things of time and sense? I fear I should neither be diligent in business nor fervent in spirit. 'But,' say you, 'he keeps talking all about himself.' True, he does; he cannot help it. Self is too much his master. I am proud of my own ignorance, and, like a toad, bloated with my own venomous pride - proud of what I have not got, and boasting when I should be bemoaning. I trust you have greater freedom from your own corruptions than I have; and in secret, social, and family prayer enjoy more blessed, sanctified liberty at the footstool of mercy.

Rejoice! for heaven awaits us, and all the Lord's family! The mansion is ready; the crown is made; the harp is strung; there are no willows there. May we be enabled to go on like lions, valiant for the truth of King Jesus, and, by the help of the Spirit, vow warfare with every sin, and rest not until the sword of the Spirit has destroyed all the enemies in our hearts.

May we be enabled to trust the Lord, for He will help us; we must conquer; we cannot be lost. Lost! Impossible! For who is able to snatch us out of our Father's hand?

May the Lord bless you exceedingly.

Your affectionate Nephew,
C. H. SPURGEON

He once said to me when I spoke to him of the value placed upon his letters by those who received them, that he did not think they would be permanently durable, as the ink he used was of a rather perishable nature; and expressed the judgment that 'there is no better ink than that to be bought in penny bottles.' His handwriting, when he was well, was singularly neat and clear; I have specimens of it that are like copper plate. Receiving contributions from nearly all parts of the world, as he constantly did, towards the work of his various institutions, it was absolutely necessary for him to have letters of grateful acknowledgment lithographed. But seldom did he send merely the lithographed form without adding at least a few sentences of grateful thanks in addition. I have several of such. Here is one sent to a dear child in the country who had with several of her companions rendered help to the Orphanage. I give the lithographed form and the added note.

Westwood, Beulah Hill, Upper Norwood: May 7, 1888

DEAR YOUNG FRIEND, - It is always very pleasant to me to receive- the help of the young. It is good to be doing good early in life. I have received the £71 15*s.* 9*d.* which you have sent me. It will help to feed the 500 little mouths of dear boys and girls who have lost their fathers.

God bless you. I thank you very much. I hope you will be the Lord's own child.

Yours heartily,
C. H. SPURGEON

This is cheering to me. I wish I could thank each one of the dear helpers personally, but I can't manage that, and so I must write - thank you, thank you, everyone! May your dear parents be spared to you, and you to them! If you ever come to London, as I hope you may, you must come to the Orphanage; I send some little books.

C. H. S.

He needed a helper in a certain department of one of his institutions once. A friend and myself suggested a name to him, and he wrote me the following:

Nightingale Lane, Balham: June 20

My DEAR MR. WILLIAMS, - Will you come over tomorrow afternoon and bring -- with you to take a cup of tea. I want to see him at once, for both you and Mr. C. think so much of him, though I fear he would never like to do the drudgery work and play second fiddle. I imagine him to be a great swell, fit to play the big bass viol, and I want more of a schoolmaster. I should, however, be glad to see him, and so would Mr. --.

Yours heartily,
C. H. SPURGEON

Send me a telegram as to whether -- can come.

I sent a telegram as follows: 'Yes, can come. Can and will play any fiddle, and keep in tune.'

On account of the reference it contains to his mother's death I give the following:

Westwood: 1888

DEAR MR. WILLIAMS, - Could you give lecture tomorrow at college at 2.30? My mother is dead, and I feel very low. If you can, please wire me first thing.

You could be done by four for your meeting.

Yours very heartily,
C. H. SPURGEON

Many of his letters written to the Church at the Tabernacle were printed with the weekly sermon, but I have one which I found on the pulpit table once when I was taking the service one Sunday evening, it having been read in the morning. I had permission to bring it away.

Westwood, Beulah Hill, Upper Norwood: 1888

DEAR FRIENDS, - When I came home yesterday from my dear mother's grave I was lame. It was raw and cold, and my knee became painful, but I had no fear. About eight o'clock torrents of pain broke over me, and the knee was soon swollen. Now I cannot put the foot on the ground, and the pain is something to remember.

Please hear my dear friend, Mr. Harrald, with thankfulness that at the eleventh hour he steps into the gap.

I send my love to you all, and great sorrow at being ill on a Sunday; but what can I do? The Lord make use of my great faggot of troubles for His own glory.

Yours sorrowfully,
C. H. SPURGEON

He heard of the illness of one of my boys, and wrote:

Westwood: April 10, 1885

DEAR FRIEND, - I am very sorry that the little boy is ill, and I earnestly trust it may not turn out to be a serious attack. What a frail creature is humanity, and especially when it is a frail specimen!

I hope the book will sell. I am all right, but full of work. Immersed to the chin in letters.

Yours heartily,
C. H. SPURGEON

Many of his letters I cannot publish - they contain personal references which were never intended to be made public; but one I received when the first difficulties of my work in London were overcome greatly cheered me, and as one or two sentences in it may do others good, I give it.

Nightingale Lane, Balham : January 1879

DEAR MR. WILLIAMS, - I rejoice at every remembrance of you. Never apologise about not sending money, your work is better than gold. Your increase as a Church is most cheering, and I think you may consider that there are better times to come, the worst of the struggle is over. Studying hard as I know you do, and living near the Lord, you will wax stronger and stronger. My heart's best blessing is upon you. I am very weak, and cannot write much.

Yours heartily,
C. H. SPURGEON

A year or two after I left college, I wrote and told him I was afraid I had better leave my Church, as a deacon and I could not get on well together, and I was afraid of a trouble in the Church. The matter, however, happily came all right, and I remained. He sent the reply facsimiled on the opposite page.

To a teacher of a Bible-class at the Tabernacle he wrote:

DEAR --, - I thank you and the class very heartily for the 10*l* for colportage. I trust every pound will really help to bring a soul to Jesus, by the colporteur's words or books.

Set the whole class praying for conversions, and ask those to give in their names who would wish to be prayed for. Sometimes this discovers an amount of secret work which else might have remained in hiding ... Peace be to you and yours. In peace will be your strength. The quiet energy, which is a sort of hiding of one's power, does much without the utter exhaustion which comes of the other method. You are learning each day, learning by the work.

Yours heartily,
C. H. SPURGEON

Upon the occasion of his jubilee, the Tabernacle Sunday school with all the teachers united in contributing to the splendid testimonial he received, but which he did not keep for himself, and he wrote thanking them thus. It was addressed to the superintendent.

To all the Tabernacle Sabbath School

Westwood: June 21, 1884

DEAR MR. PEARCE, - I salute you as the Captain of the Host below stairs and in the college. Peace be to you, and to all your helpers. Brethren and sisters beloved, I value your affection above rubies, and I breathe my prayers to heaven that all covenant

Nightingale Lane
Clapham
Feb 5-

Bear. Bear. Bear.
Forbear. Forbear. Forbear

In yielding is victory
Fight the devil & love the
deacon — Love him till
he is loveable

Yours heartily
C H Spurgeon

blessings may be yours.

Dear young ones who are saved, the Lord keep you, and ripen your graces, and gladden your hearts.

Dear boys and girls, not yet saved, the silver trumpets of Jubilee invite you to come to Jesus today. The sooner you trust the Lord Jesus, the sooner you will be happy, safe, and holy. Believe in Him and live. You will be worthy men and women if you become believing children. Why not? Jesus is ready to receive you.

May the school be a model to all England of true graciousness. You have the dearest superintendent that ever lived, and some of the choicest teachers yet on earth. May all dear children among you love the Lord; may all do so at once, for *He* deserves it.

You have all united to make me glad. The Lord God Almighty bless you all at this hour.

Your loving Pastor,
C. H. SPURGEON

During his last illness a letter was sent to the pastor from the superintendent of the Sunday school, telling him of a successful annual meeting of the Loan Tract Society, and also of the fact that some boys in the Sunday school had said they were praying for his recovery every day. His reply was:

Menton: December 12, 1891

My DEAR FRIEND, - Your very sweet letter added another flower to this garden of the sun. Bless the Lord for His goodness to the Tract Society. Assure all the workers that I joy in their rejoicing.

The school is always a fruitful field, and it makes me happy to think of the boys and girls praying for me. Perhaps a special plea from them may quicken the pace of my recovery, which is very tardy at present. I am sure I am better, but I am sadly weak, and if anyone talks to me too much, or I read or write a little more than usual, I feel how great my weakness is.

The school has done well for missions. Give my love to all the teachers. I know of no exception; they are all dear to me. The superintendent is, however, specially dear. God bless *him* and *his*.

Yours always heartily,
C. H. SPURGEON

I have two other letters of much earlier date than the above, which tell of his esteem and love for the Sunday school and its teachers.

Menton: March 12, 1879

DEAR FRIEND, - It gave me great rest when you undertook the Sabbath school, and my joy was great when I saw how the teachers rallied round you. I thank you very heartily, and I bless God for all that has been done by you in uniting the school and leading it on to success.

Thank all the teachers and helpers for your noble contribution to the bazaar. The Lord return into their own bosoms their loving deed towards their pastor, who feels deeply indebted to them, and blesses them in the name of the Lord.

As to the excursions - you know best. I am so little aware of the cost and your means of meeting it that I do not like to give a judgment. We found the matter too costly aforetime, and thought the money could be better spent. I remain much of the same mind now, but I do not feel myself qualified to give an opinion. Select some place which can be reached cheaply, and where there can be some keeping of the children to themselves. The mixed multitude with former excursions caused me many reflections, and made me glad that they were abandoned. Still, evils being avoided, a holiday does the dear children good. Do as your wisdom directs. May the Lord be with you ever, and may your heart be comforted in this good work.

Yours, with Christian love,
C. H. SPURGEON

Nightingale Lane, Balham: May 10, 1879

DEAR MR. --, - As the time draws near for giving me the testimonial, I am anxious to thank you and all the teachers for your noble share therein. It was done so spontaneously and so liberally that it touches my heart all the more. God bless you all, and give you your children as your wages, and His own smile as your daily refreshment. Your unity delights me, and I believe it will ensure a rich blessing, for there the Lord commandeth it, where brethren dwell together in unity. I propose to have an evening with you all, and with the teachers of the other contributing schools. I think we could make it pleasant and profitable. I must see you soon as to an evening. A Friday will suit me best.

Yours ever heartily,
C. H. SPURGEON

The following letter is to the same:

Westwood: May 26, 1888

DEAR FRIEND, - The Lord bless you in the work of your hands, and soon set you free. I hope the liver will wake up. I am in seas of trouble, but the Lord High Admiral is on board. I will aid you as to books for Sunday school, and in any other way you desire.

Yours very lovingly,
C. H. SPURGEON

To one of his most earnest helpers he wrote:

Westwood: June 24, 1884

DEAR --, I was truly sorry to hear of your illness, but Elijah must faint if he runs before the chariot, and who is to prevent his running? I don't wonder at your excitement, or blame you, but I do feel sad that it should lead to such illness, and place you in such great danger. You are a splendid engine, but you will burst up if you are worked at such high pressure. The most of our people need the fire to be poked, and very rarely do we need to be damped down; but you, dear --, are not so strong as you look to be, and must be careful.

Anyhow, we will rejoice together. The Lord hath done great things for us; whereof we are glad. Peace be unto you. The sycamore fig was bruised before it became sweet. The bruising has been done with heavy hand; but the sweetness is evidently coming. The Lord bless both you and dear --. I am deeply grateful to you both for the generous present sent to me, which is the most personal gift I have received. I fear it rejoices a weakness, but it is certainly all my own.

Yours heartily,
C. H. SPURGEON

Gratitude breathes in nearly all his letters. The following one sent as an acknowledgment for a cheque for 30*l.* for his work is characteristic of his deep and ceaseless appreciation of the generosity of God's people.

Nightingale Lane, Clapham: Dec. 28

DEAR FRIEND, - Until today I have not been able to sit down to letters, and knowing you were out, I felt I might delay. You are very generous to our work. The Lord ever bless you in pocket as well as in heart. I don't know what blessing to invoke upon you and your beloved, 'for all things are yours.' May you evermore abide in Christ Jesus in fulness of joy. I hope I may see you soon and thank you by word of mouth. Till then to yourself and husband I desire my love in Christ Jesus.

Yours gratefully,
C. H. SPURGEON

Acknowledging a gift from a Bible class, he wrote:
All in the class meet their beloved leader in heaven! Will they?
Writing from Mentone to a friend in England he says:

DEAR FRIEND, - I am very sorry that Mr. -- is so ill. It is very warm here, and intensely dry. It would do great good to a cold or influenza, only the task is to get here. May our Lord bless you both wherever you are, and sanctify slight afflictions as well as great ones. I feel so much better that I hardly know myself. My spirits are now elastic, and the heart is singing all day long. The burden is taken from the shoulder and the labouring ox ruminates. My love to Mr. -- and yourself as dear friends in Christ Jesus.

Yours heartily,
C. H. SPURGEON

We hope to be here another week.

When recovering from an attack of gout at Mentone he thus wrote to a friend in England:
DEAR --, ... I am well, but weak. My feet are gradually giving up the evil habit of being 'puffed up,' but they renounce this natural tendency of humanity with evident reluctance. So I fear I am not

quite right yet, especially as one knee gave in yesterday, and to be weak on the knees is terrible for a minister.

The weather has been mixed; but today we are able to go out, and I feel rising like the barometer.

I trust the troubles of -- will be laid at the Master's feet, and then made light of. I am thankful they are no worse.

To you and to -- I send not as a compliment, but in all earnest Christian love, my hearty salutation, wishing you a better year than you have ever had. *A year of Our Lord* in capital letters.

Yours ever most heartily,
C. H. SPURGEON

When recovering from one illness he wrote me, 'I am better, but weak, and sometimes low. This is my worst feature.' Only those who saw his sufferings knew how utterly low his spirits were often brought.

To a valued Christian worker who was ill he once wrote:

Menton

DEAR --, ... I felt grieved to note how ill you seem to be, only kept up by your indomitable spirit. I am afraid you may undertake too much, and break down yet further under the strain. Better serve the Lord with five talents than kill yourself with trying to make them seven.

Mr. -- must have preached well, if I may judge his sermon by your extract. We have a nice company of some twenty-four to prayer each morning. The weather is perfect. Only Mr. and Mrs. -- are with me.

May heaven's own smile light up house and heart for you while the husband is away. Salem.

Yours ever heartily,
C. H. SPURGEON

The next letter I deem to be *one* of the most choice I have ever seen written by him. The handwriting is singularly neat, and as beautiful as the contents.

Hôtel Beau Rivage: December 15

DEAR FRIEND, - Your kind note has reached me and cheered me. I had eight sunny days here, and then the dragon overtook me and cast me down. Just as I thought I would write you my enemy struck me in the right arm, so that I could not hold a pen or write a word. Moreover, I was unable to do or to think. Since then both feet have been imperial in colour, improper in proportions, and impotent for motion. This is now the third week of my sickness, but things are brighter. I can write, as you see, and I can walk across a room, and I can think, and I can trust, and not be afraid. Bless the Lord with me.

I pray that you may be preserved in all your goings. We have had the finest imaginable weather. Mr. Alabaster leaves me tomorrow, and I expect Mr. Passmore today.

Things seem quietly alive at home. I thank you much for remembering my dear wife, who toils and slaves while I luxuriate, or might do, if I were well. That dear - of yours, God bless him. May you both have a quiet, happy time. Go at half speed. Don't make camels and donkeys go like racehorses. I think of you both with loving gratitude, and would like to see you.

I try to go out a little ride, but it blows today, and so I shall be a prisoner. God is very gracious to me. I am now enrolled in the work-and-suffer corps, and expect to have double grace for the double part I am to sustain. Pray it may be so. Write again.

Yours ever most heartily,
C. H. SPURGEON

In a certain family there are several bearing the names of Old Testament worthies; this explains the following letter, which Mr. Spurgeon wrote to one of this household.

Westwood: August 30, 1890

DEAR MR. --, - What a patriarchal family you are: here is Joshua sending me a letter from Noah, containing news about Enoch and Job and his girls. It makes me feel proud to be in such ancient company.

God bless you all. I will send Noah a receipt. Like his namesake, he seems to have had enough rain.

Well, we shall get home. You are a good soul. May the Lord give you the double portion, as He did Job!

Yours heartily ever,
C. H. SPURGEON

The following was a reply written on a postcard to the request made to him that he would, as 'John Ploughman,' write something on the Disestablishment question for the Liberation Society:

Clapham: November 17, 1870

DEAR Sir, - John Ploughman is just now up to his neck in other work, and his pen, picked off the common, is a very irregular quill. Sometimes the ink runs, and sometimes it doesn't. However, the matter will be thought over, and if a fountain flows you will see an outpouring in the *Sword and Trowel*, and we will then talk about what to do with it. J. P. would be pleased to do the work just when you want it, but his ways are disorderly; he cannot work to order. His thoughts, like the partridges, are decidedly wild, and can't be shot down when he wants them.

Yours truly,
C. H. SPURGEON

When Messrs. Fullerton and Smith were conducting services at the Tabernacle upon one occasion the pastor wrote:

Marseilles: Wednesday Noon

We have arrived here happily, after travelling all night. I am very frequently thinking of you and the work at the Tabernacle. Send me word to Mentone, where I hope to be tomorrow (Thursday). May some of the lapstones be broken: I have not many, but the few are hard. May some of the rolling stones be fixed in the temple wall. May adamant become flesh. May flint be taken quite away. May the Lord Jesus be to thousands the headstone of the corner. Who else should be? Where else would they put Him? My love to all my beloved fellow workers and yourselves.

Yours very heartily,
C. H. SPURGEON

Here is a reply he sent to one who wrote asking questions relative to certain matters of doctrine.

Westwood: March 15, 1887

DEAR FRIEND, - As to Hebrews, I have always taught that if the Divine life could entirely die out there would be no second quickening. We can be born again, but not again and again. If the salt could lose its savour, it would be a hopeless case. From which I argue that, as no man is in a hopeless case, no man has utterly lost the life of God after once receiving it.

The wilful return to sin would be fatal.

In each passage quoted the evil supposed is also denied. See Heb. vi. 9; Heb. x. 39.

One great means of securing final perseverance is the knowledge that we cannot go in and out of Christ at pleasure: if we could utterly quit Him, there could be no possibility of renewal. Heb. vi. 4. Therefore we are bound to hold on even to the end.

My wonder is how, in the teeth of these texts, Arminians believe men to lose the Divine life and receive it again. No words can be clearer than those which describe this as impossible.

I have sent a catalogue with sermons marked which may help you. Write me whenever you like, only excuse me if I am brief.

Yours heartily,
C. H. SPURGEON

The following letter written to the same inquirer deals with a matter of permanent interest.

Westwood: April 1, 1882

DEAR FRIEND, - I am the earnest friend and helper of all who preach the Gospel of Jesus; yet I deem it no unfriendly thing to speak the truth, and what I wrote in 1876 I have never seen any reason to alter. Messrs. Moody and Sankey are two blessed men of God, and if their converts on that occasion vanished it was no fault of theirs, neither would I have had them refrain for an hour - far from it.

The movement in London had comparatively no link with the Churches, and fostered a rival spirit, and hence it did not bring a permanent blessing of increase to the Churches. Still it brought a great blessing to the Church Universal, and revived and encouraged us all.

I would warn Churches against *trusting* in spasmodic effort, but at the same time against refusing such special help as the Lord puts in their way. There is a medium.

In any case I am not *against* evangelistic effort, but heartily its advocate.

Yours very truly and gratefully,
C. H. SPURGEON

To one of his Church officers he wrote:

Menton: Wednesday

DEAR MR. --, - I have a cold upon me, and have had to keep in, but I am much improving through the rest and warmth of this place. I wish you all a merry Christmas. The Lord be with all the deacons and elders in their holy gatherings … I trust all will go well. I fear I shall need a week or so more than I at first proposed, since I lost a fortnight by being taken ill. I wish I could be always well, and I have denied myself much to gain it; but I must bow before the Divine will, and do my best. I look up with prayerful faith to our great Father to bless the Church in my absence, and make my absence as little injurious as may be … May the Lord bless the preaching, and glorify His name in His own people.

Go and see Mrs.--. If she needs anything, I should be glad to supply it; but you can hardly mention it to her. Please find out in a side way. I hope you and your household are well.

Yours very heartily,
C. H. SPURGEON

Many were the letters he wrote at different times which speak of the great pain he suffered and of his enforced absence on account of illness.

Westwood: November 4, 1890

DEAR MR. --, - I am sorry to miss seeing you and - and my venerable and beloved friend Canon Hussey; but I have had to keep my bed, my restless bed; and to suffer remarkable pain, a sort of cramp in the neck and other neuralgic agonies. I am spun out. I am sitting up to write this note, and send my love to you all, and you must half smile when I say that it is a painful effort to write even these few words.

God be with you, one and all. Pray for a poor prisoner.

C. H. SPURGEON

Westwood: April 27, 1891

DEAR FRIENDS, - The excessive strain of the week seemed suddenly to come upon me when I stood before the people on Sunday night. My mouth seemed to become dry, so that my teeth would not keep their place, and my heart failed me with a fear of which I felt ashamed, but which I could not overcome. I have been so busy and so happy that I felt a sudden reaction, and broke down. Don't be at all distressed about me. I shall soon be right. Indeed, I fancy I could preach now; but I must keep still this week, and be ready for next Sunday, if the Lord will. You will bear with me a little longer, and when I grow too old and feeble you must find some one else.

Yours ever lovingly,
C. H. SPURGEON

To be read at prayer meeting. Mr. Frank Smith will be there, let him speak.

Westwood: 1888, Sabbath Evening

DEAR FRIENDS, - As you love me, pray for me specially just now. Never did I need your prayers more. Could you meet with one another to plead with God for me that I may be directed and sustained? The times are evil, and the trial for the Man of God peculiar.

I am not well, but it will soon pass off, and I hope speedily to be in full work. My teeth are troubling me just now, but if I once get over this, and my bodily weakness goes off, I shall be up to the mark soon, by God's grace.

I am what and where I always have been in testimony to the truth. We shall as a Church and people have to bear our witness for the Lord, and He will not fail us.

Oh that all of you may be aroused to pray, and bring the people in to hear the Word, and to endeavour to win souls for Jesus. Again, with deepest love to you, I say 'Pray.'

Your tired Pastor,
C. H. SPURGEON

To a Bible class he wrote:

Westwood: January 18, 1888

DEAR BRETHREN, - The Lord bless you. I have no greater joy than this - to see my children in Christ walking in the truth. 'Ye are strong, and have overcome the wicked one.' You love the glorious Gospel, live upon it, and let it live in you more and more. Many of you are now well established by experience, and you can strengthen the younger sort. Be all of you ready to stand up for Jesus in this evil day. I see all around us not only error and unbelief, but also mad fanaticism. Only those who are established in the faith will be able to endure in the hour of trial. That the Lord's truth will conquer is sure. Oh that we may be partakers in that victory! ... The Lord make the class more and more an army of the Lord, and a training school for workers. I invoke upon you the infinite benediction of the Triune.

Yours most heartily,
C. H. SPURGEON

The following was sent to a beloved elder of the Tabernacle.

Menton: February 24, 1877

DEAR MR. --, ... I am astonished and delighted at the work which you have all done, and at the wise manner in which everything has been arranged with a view to variety and interest. Some of you have worked very hard, and I earnestly hope that our beloved brother -- has not gone too far, as he is very apt to do in his holy fervour ... I have had one bad night, but otherwise I am wonderfully well, though that one night of misery makes me almost fear a return. The sun shines always here, and we have very warm days, and never a drop of rain by any chance.

Lend all the aid in your power to the Sunday school, which is, I fear, passing through a trying ordeal. Mr.- has all my confidence and esteem, and I feel sure that all will work for the best.

May the abiding blessing of the Lord rest on you all. Please give the enclosed notes to the students. Some ten out of the whole body have written as I requested, and I have answered them all. It is now too late for any more to write me, as I start home on Monday.

Yours ever heartily,
C. H. SPURGEON

To the same.

Menton: December 21

DEAR --, - This is a Sabbath with us, but not a S*un*day. It is grey and windy, and I am not able to go out. Yet I am much better, although my middle finger is only middling, and will not let the gout go out.

The small punning which appears above is solely due to your letter. I am not in the habit of committing puns, but there is a contagion about persons who have the evil in its very worst form ... I desire you to tender my kindest love to each one of the elders ... I thank those who pray for me. In my pain and weakness I have had great need of your prayers, and now that I am getting well I feel it even more.

Oh for a great blessing! I open my mouth wide, and there is the promise, 'I will fill it.'

The weather is unsettled here, and cold for this place. The logs of olive blaze cheerfully, and are a necessity.

Remember me to --. Peace be unto you! I cannot write more - the finger forbids.

Yours heartily,
C. H. SPURGEON

Menton: Monday

DEAR --, - It must be very bad to be at home, for winter has reached us here. To our surprise we found it snowing one evening, and a mere dust remained till morning on the pavement. The sun is clouded, and when that is the case the glory is departed. Same with the soul. I cannot get out to walk, for I cannot move fast enough to keep warm. This is a hindrance to me. This morning I went a ride in my great-coat. It is sad to see how vegetation here has felt the frost - palms, oranges, lemons look shrivelled, and the herbs and plants and flowers many of them are killed - that is to say, the tender sort. Peas in bloom look as if they could not tell whether to die or not, and broad beans the same. I enclose a cheque for 10*l.* for the poor either in or out of the Church, through yourself or any of the societies which will spend it at once during the cold.

I have from thirty to fifty to my family prayer each morning, filling my sitting-room and bedroom. The Lord is blessing His Word, and I am helped in preparing for work at home ... Love to every elder. It is very gracious of the Lord to spare them, but I fear some hold on with difficulty in the fog and frost. I am looking forward to my return with great pleasure. I hope -- are as well as weather allows.

Yours ever truly,
C. H. SPURGEON

Westwood: June 21, 1884

To the Holy Band at -

DEAR FRIENDS ALL, - Thank you heartily. I bless God when I think of Captain --, and all the noble warriors who fight for our Lord at --. May the King Himself be ever in your midst, and consequent prosperity.

While yet the silver sounds of the jubilee trumpets linger in the air, I salute you all with great love. The Lord recompense you. To each one I send my hearty affection.

Yours in the Lord,
C. H. SPURGEON

Menton: January 23

DEAR FRIEND, - ... I have had sharp pains, but I am recovering. Only my back is broken, and I need a new vertebrae. I feel delighted in the prospect of coming home, though this is a dry, bright, sunny, paradisiacal place …I preached on Sunday from 'Your joy no man taketh from you.' All our brethren know that treasure - that joy. Let us be as joyful as the angels.

Your loving friend,
C. H. SPURGEON

I have on my study table a letter dated January 15, 1892. This must be among the last he wrote. Mr. W. Higgs has a postcard dated January 20, but I know of no letter of later date than the 15th. The one I possess deals with a purely private and personal matter, and so cannot be printed, but in it he says:

'The bad weather does not help me. Never mind, we shall see brighter times before long. Roman capital … I cannot write. I feel tired with being indoors.'

The brighter times soon came, brighter even than he anticipated. The earliest letter I have is one dated June 11, 1856, in which he calls a meeting of certain gentlemen members of Park Street, 'to confer upon the best course of action for providing increased accommodation for the congregation who attend with us.'

In one letter which I possess he tells he had with the boys in the Orphanage of a happy time It is dated

Westwood: September 24, 1890

DEAR FRIEND ,- One cold gone and No. 2 going. Had a happy hour yesterday in the Orphanage play hall in an awful storm, with the boys all around me. I talked to them, and between the peals of thunder they sang and I prayed. I believe they were greatly impressed. It was a very solemn time ….

I feel very wearied, and I am glad that I am working my way towards a rest.

Yours ever lovingly,
C. H. SPURGEON

With a letter addressed to the ministers in view of the Conference I bring this chapter to a close. It shows how intensely he longed for the Conference week to be a season of real blessing, and how earnestly he prayed it might be so. In this letter we have much of the secret of those pentecostal days we year by year enjoyed.

Metropolitan Tabernacle, Newington, S.E.: March 4,1887

My DEAR FRIEND, - As the time for the College Conference draws nigh I am full of anxiety, and I would desire to let that anxiety condense into prayer. Please join me in that prayer.

Our sole desire is the glory of God, and this would be greatly promoted if we all made a distinct advance in the Divine life: this may be produced by the Holy Spirit through our communion with each other and the Lord. Let us bow low before the throne for this, and take hold upon the promises with a mighty faith.

It is comparatively a small matter to all but myself; but I hunger to be with you all the day every day. We love each other in the Lord, and yet see so little of each other that I am bitterly disappointed if taken from you by pain. Brother, pray that we may look each other in the face, and may together behold our Lord. Would you do me the great service to set apart a little time privately to seek an unusual blessing? and it would be a great gain if in addition you could lead your Church to pray with us. I pine for a heavenly shower to saturate us all.

Please answer the letters of secretaries promptly. This is a huge business: ease us all you can.

Your loving friend,
C. H. SPURGEON

CHAPTER VIII

THE FAMOUS PREACHER

A HIGH Church paper, recently reviewing two volumes of Mr. Spurgeon's sermons, remarked, 'We have often dwelt upon the sermons of Mr. Spurgeon as being worthy of the closest study on the part of the young preacher, and as we close these two books we are again moved to urge homiletical students to leave commonplace volumes of sermons alone, and to study only the great masters of pulpit eloquence. In Mr. Spurgeon they will find a gift of plain speech which has never been surpassed in the pulpits of English Nonconformity." Years ago Paxton Hood wrote: 'It may be safely affirmed that never, in any period of the history of the Church, did any man rise and hold in sustained attention and active Christian useful labour a weekly congregation, certainly not numbering less than from 5,000 to 6,000 persons, with no popular prestige, no music to aid, no robes to give effect, no ceremonials of service, plain, simple, and unadorned.'

A few personal reminiscences of some sermons of the gifted preacher will doubtless prove interesting to many. I have in my library nearly ninety volumes, in addition to the *Sword and Trowel*, which Mr. Spurgeon issued from the press; and most of these consist of sermons delivered in the ordinary course of his ministry. There must be connected with very many of these sermons a history, gracious, fascinating, and even romantic. I count myself happy to be able to write a few interesting facts connected with some of them.

On May 30, 1857, a brother minister was standing with Mr. Spurgeon under a tree. The atmosphere was so calm and still that scarcely a leaf trembled; suddenly a gentle zephyr stirred the leaves above their heads, then there was a rustling sound. Mr. Spurgeon suddenly interrupted the conversation with, 'Stop! keep quiet! don't speak! - there! my sermon for tomorrow; "The sound of a going in the tops of the mulberry trees."' The friend looked up and saw they were standing under a mulberry tree. The sermon was preached on the following evening. It is printed, and is No. 317 in the weekly series. A gentleman who served as deacon at the Tabernacle for many years, but who has been dead some time, told me that this sermon won him to the Saviour. I took the same subject when in my first pastorate, and (as the reader would surmise, even if I did not confess) was greatly helped in the preparation by reading what Mr. Spurgeon had first preached and then printed, though I can say the sermon was honestly my own. A father, mother, two sons and a daughter, in one family, joined the Church as a result of my discourse on the mulberry tree. I told Mr. Spurgeon this.

A Presbyterian minister once expressed to me his conviction that the best sermon in the earlier volumes is the one entitled 'False Professors solemnly warned.' It is certainly a model as to arrangement, and exhibits a glow of spiritual fervour and intensity to a greater degree than many others. It is in Vol. ii. of the *New Park Street Pulpit*, No. 102. A careful perusal of it cannot but help any young minister or student.

A leading Baptist minister gave it as his judgment that the sermon entitled 'Things that accompany Salvation' is the most eloquent, and exhibits greater mental power than any Mr. Spurgeon ever delivered. It is perhaps as eloquent as any published, but in later volumes there are sermons of even greater ability. I was with Mr. Spurgeon on Saturday, August 25, 1883. He was exceedingly unwell, his arms were rigid with rheumatic gout, and the pain he endured was little less than torture. The Tabernacle was being renovated, and he was preaching in the meantime in Exeter Hall. My church also was under repair; I was free on Sunday mornings, and preached in the evenings in the Canterbury Theatre; so he said, 'Mr. Williams, I am afraid there is little prospect of my being able to preach tomorrow. You be at Exeter Hall with a sermon ready, in case I cannot.' He did come, however. It was a brave deed. He had the utmost difficulty in opening the Bible and turning over its leaves. Yet on that morning, with bent form, and with countenance drawn and distorted with pain, he delivered a sermon worthy to rank among the masterpieces of pulpit eloquence. The text was, 'Talk no more so exceeding proudly; let not arrogancy come out of your mouth: for the Lord is a God of knowledge, and by Him actions are weighed,' I Samuel ii. 3. The sermon is printed under the title 'The King's Weighings,' and its number is 1,736. Let the reader obtain it, and he will conclude with us that the great preacher increased in mental strength as years increased. It has the fervour of his youth and the wisdom and strength of a ripened and matured manhood. But the oratorical power of 'Things that accompany Salvation' shows to what heights of eloquence, what flights of imagination he was capable of rising. He growingly sought to suppress this style of delivery, 'and counted that, as he told the students, 'the perfection of preaching is to talk it.'

 I once expressed to him my judgment that the sermons in volumes from 1860 to 1867 are not up to the uniformly high level of the earlier or later ones. Some sermons in these volumes have exceptional power; but the high average of power I considered was scarcely maintained. 'Yes,' he said, 'I think it may be so.' It is to be accounted for by the fact that his style was undergoing a change; and that in the place of the dashing cataract and leaping torrent of eloquence there was the ever-deepening, ever widening flow of a refreshing river of instruction. During the earliest years of his ministry he preached to gather a congregation, and having gathered it, to interest the people and win them to God. Speaking of his ministry in the Music Hall of the Royal Surrey Gardens he said, 'In that edifice I have such a congregation, and so diversified, as few men ever had regularly to minister to. God only knows what anxiety I have experienced in selecting my subjects and arranging my appeals for such a vast fluctuating assembly. There was a time when my brain whirled at the very thought of ascending that pulpit.' But having gathered a great Church and settled down in his own house of worship, he sought more and more, with quiet yet undiminished power, to lead his flock into the green pastures and beside the still waters of Divine truth.

In the volume of sermons for 1859, No. 227, there is one sermon specially remarkable. It is entitled 'Compel them to come in.' Years ago I had it, either from Mr. Spurgeon himself or from one of the officers at the Tabernacle, that at least three hundred joined the Church who attributed their conversion to that sermon. In reading it one cannot wonder that it was so, for neither in the sermons of Whitefield nor Baxter is the art of pleading with men seen to greater perfection. Let preachers who would be soul winners turn to it, and read it again and again, and it may be that they also will learn how to become masters of this most precious of all arts.

How I wish I could win men;
For 'mid all life's quests there seems but worthy one -
To do men good.

In many a heart this wish will find an echo. Of the sermon itself Mr. Spurgeon wrote, 'The sermon entitled "Compel them to come in" has been so signally owned of God, that scarcely a week occurs without some case of its usefulness coming to light. The violent, rigid school of Calvinists will, of course, abhor the sermon: but this is a very small matter when the Holy Ghost works by it in the salvation of men. Would to God that such a prolific discourse could be preached every day in the week, or rather, would that every effort had a like benediction resting upon it!'

There are three volumes of Mr. Spurgeon's early sermons, entitled The Pulpit Library, now out of print and seldom to be found. I have two of the series, but have never been able to obtain the third, though I have seen it. These consist for the most part of sermons delivered soon after he came to London, on Sunday and Thursday evenings. The first sermon in Vol. ii., on the text, 'Prove me now,' Malachi iii. 10, was preached at New Park Street on the morning of the Lord's Day on which the fatal accident occurred at the Surrey Music Hall. Of it the author says: 'By many it will now be perused with curiosity, but the preacher himself reviews each sentence with thrilling emotion. Its subject was entirely suggested by the enlarged sphere of labour he was about to occupy, and the then unprecedented number of souls he was expecting ere nightfall to address. If any passage seem to forestall the calamity, he can only say it is genuine - a transcript from the reporter's notes.' Whether the calamity be forestalled or not, the sermon, read in the light of that terrible fact, contains some remarkable passages. In the discourse he says: 'To allegorise a moment. There is a ship upon the sea. It is the ship which the Lord has launched, and which He said should come to its desired haven. The sea is smooth; the waves ripple gently, and bear the bark steadily along. "Prove me now," saith the Lord. The mariner stands on the deck and says, "Lord, I thank Thee that Thou hast given me such smooth sailing as this; but, ah, my Master, perhaps this very ease and comfort may destroy my grace." A voice says, "Prove Me now, and see if I cannot keep thee amidst the storm." Anon the heavens have gathered blackness, the winds have begun to bluster, and the waves lift up their voice, while the poor ship is tossed to and fro on the yawning deep. Amid the screaming of the tempest and the howling of the winds I hear a voice which says, "Prove Me now." See, the ship is on the rock. She has been dashed upon it; she has been broken well nigh in sunder, and the mariner sees her hold filling with water, while all his pumps cannot keep her empty. The voice still cries, "Prove Me now." Alas! she well nigh sinks; and the waves will swamp her; it seems as if one more drop would submerge her. Still the voice cries, "Prove Me now." And the mariner does prove God, and he is delivered safely from all his distresses.' And again, *'See what God can do, just when a cloud is falling on the head of him whom God has raised up to preach to you.'*

I remember, when in college, our venerable and revered tutor, Mr. Rogers, gave us a lecture on the art of allegro rising. Among other sources of illustration from which he drew examples of the art was a sermon by Mr. Spurgeon on 'The Parable of the Ark.' I find this sermon in the same volume of *The Pulpit Library* as 'Prove Me now.' It is singularly ingenious and clever, and must have enchanted those who listened to it on its first delivery. It seems a pity it was not included in the *New Park Street Pulpit*. From the fact that there was only one window in the Ark, the preacher proceeds to show that 'all who come to Christ and receive salvation are illuminated in one way. The one window of the Ark may fitly represent to us the ministry of the Holy Ghost ... "Why," says one, "there are some of us who see light through one minister and some through another." True, my friend: but still there is only one window. We ministers are like panes of glass and you can obtain no light through us but by the operations of the same Spirit that worketh in us. And even then the different panes of glass give different shades of light. There you have your fine polished preacher; he is a bit of stained glass, not very transparent, made to keep the light out rather than to let it in. There is another pane; he is a square-cut diamond; he seems an old fashioned preacher, but still he is a bit of good glass, and lets the light through. Another one is cut after a more refined style: but still he is plain and simple, and the light shines through him. But still there is only one light, and only one window. He Who revealeth to us the light of the knowledge of the glory of God in the face of Jesus Christ is the Holy Spirit.' The sermon must be read as a whole to be appreciated. In it there is a distinct indication of that power of felicity of illustration and wondrous imagination which helped to make so many of his subsequent discourses a charm to the minds and an inspiration to the hearts of multitudes.

There are several other sermons in these volumes of singular beauty and strength. One, delivered on the preacher's birthday, on 'What is your Life?' another on 'Meditation'; another on 'Death a Sleep.' A gentleman of sound judgment, who has read Mr. Spurgeon's sermons for many years, told me, the other day, he considered that Mr. Spurgeon never excelled these earliest productions. I did not agree with him; but some of them are doubtless masterpieces, and stand in all sermon literature absolutely unrivalled as the productions of a youth of but twenty years. John

Calvin's Institutes, published when he was twenty-eight; Ruskin's Modern Painters, published when he was twenty-four; Bailey's Festus, published when he was twenty-three; and Spurgeon's first volume of sermons

> These first-fruits bring I; nor do thou forego
> Marking, when I the feat thus closed, began,
> Which numbers now three years from its plan,
> Not twenty summers had embrowned my brow.
> Life at a blood-heat every page doth prove,
> Bear with it. Nature means Necessity.
>
> DEDICATION, in *Festus*

published when he was twenty-one, stand out as four of the greatest examples of youthful genius contained in any literature. What it must have been to hear these sermons delivered, No wonder that New Park Street soon became crowded to suffocation; that not only Exeter Hall filled and the Strand became blocked when he preached there; but that the Great Surrey Music Hall should be filled with 10,000 people at half-past ten on a dull November Sunday morning, waiting for him as the thirsty earth for the rain; and that another 10,000 should be outside, seeking admission in vain.

Of scores, I may almost say hundreds, of the sermons of later years I know the origin. Let me tell the reader a little of what I know. Here is a facsimile of a sermon outline from which he preached the sermon entitled 'Gathering to the Centre,' on Lord's Day morning, June 4, 1876, No. 1,298.

The week before he had been taking a few days' rest at Ockley, his favourite spot in Surrey. Two miles from the village is Okewood Church, which he went to see. It was his usual custom and growing pleasure to visit village churches and churchyards when opportunity offered. I visited this same choice spot with him some time after the visit he made in 1876. He pointed out the peculiar feature of five or six different paths through the churchyard, and all converging to a point at the church door, and said: 'It was from this I got my sermon on the text, "They came to Him from every quarter," Mark i. 45.'

A recent visit to Okewood, for the purpose of obtaining some pictures of 'the very rustic church which stands embowered in a wood,' has afforded me much pleasure. It recalled the happy seasons spent in the neighbourhood with Mr. Spurgeon, and gave me an opportunity of beholding once more one of the fairest spots in our own fair Surrey.

Imagination would find it difficult to picture a more enchanting region. Extensive woods once covered the hills and dales for many miles round; but the luxuriant remains of these afford ample opportunity for quiet seclusion and delightful repose. Cowper, who in his mental weariness sighed for

> A lodge in some vast wilderness,
> Some boundless continuity of shade,

could well have been content to dwell in this sequestered and tranquil spot. Ockley village has itself no mean attraction for such as seek a really quiet rural resting-place; but to drive from Ockley to Okewood through Nature's own avenues, and beneath her living arches of oak, and beech, and chestnut, and then to rusticate in the shady dells hard by where the little church nestles, brings a balm to a tired brain such as only a whisper from God could do to a stricken heart. The day was in early June when I and two friends were there. Several fields were one mass of rich colour; this the marguerite

~ Mark I. 45

In the literal fact there is encouragement. Jesus draws a congregation — let us preach him to draw. But it is Jesus healing, the results of the gospel attract. Personal testimony is the grand advertisement. The people will come from every quarter.

From this great outer circle some were drawn into the central ring — these of every kind. Fishermen, a Pharisee, a publican, a physician, honourable women. The fact however may also be used as typical.

I. <u>Of the open or professional coming</u>
  Some from lower motives of self-seeking. Loaves.
  Some from admiration of his eloquence. Blessed is the womb &c
  Some moved by transient enthusiasm. Stony ground
  Some with much ignorance of his character. No leave when more is told.
  Some come from sincere conviction
  Some are traitors as was Judas.

II. <u>Of the first real spiritual coming</u>
  The church in the wood sits from pallies
  From low grounds of deep despair
  From high grounds of self-esteem
  From bewilderment & doubt
  From earnest seeking & endeavouring.
  He little knows us of the ways they come but he does
    he dwells there he sees them a great way off
  Let us pray for them & help them
  Of all who come no one is disappointed
  He casts out none. The greater no prejudice.
  He is honoured & gladdened by every one.
  There is no fear of their leaving off coming.
    his attractions never fail.
  Yet are there some who pause by the way & rest short of him   Alas!

III. Of the daily comings of saved souls.
Of outward circumstances in life, rank &c
    trial & joy.
Of mental pursuits   Jerusalem
Of theological thought   London —
Of spiritual emotion
Of spiritual characteristic. Ind. Acknl,
Of spiritual growth
Here then is the common meeting place.
To him sh⟨oul⟩d we be path-makers
We sh⟨oul⟩d prize Him because he is so full of
    blessing to others.
We sh⟨oul⟩d commune together concerning him
    seeing we all view him from
    different points —

IV. Of the final coming
From all ages, places, ranks, conditions
From unlikely quarters. Sin, error, superstition
All to Him! What meetings.
The universe meets in him. Angels, doves, deer
drinking, lion, rabbit.. Material & spiritual
Christ is all. The gathering together in One in Him

416 National Anthem.
425 Boston
436 Stephens. —

claims as her own queenly domain, and this the golden buttercup; while over yonder the red clover, baptized in the blushing sunshine, seems like a waveless sea of fire; and in the meadow near our feet the modest daisies in countless thousands - as though roused to jealousy by their neighbours' colours - emblems of the empyreal and the pure - seemed to lift their heads and say, 'Are not we too worthy to be admired and praised?'

>Ye bright mosaics, that with storied beauty
>This floor of Nature's temple tesselate,
>What numerous lessons of instructive duty
>Your forms create!

>'Neath cloistered bough, each floral bell that swingeth
>And tolls its perfume on the passing air,
>Makes Sabbath in the fields, and ever ringeth
>A call to prayer.

>Floral apostles, that with dewy splendour
>Blush without sin, and weep without a crime;
>O! may I deeply learn, and ne'er surrender
>Your lore divine.

While gazing on this fair panorama of natural loveliness notes of music borne on a gentle zephyr entrance our ears:

>'Tis the merry nightingale
>That crowds, and hurries, and precipitates
>With fast thick warble his delicious notes.
>And now the blackbird's whistle and the throstle's song are heard,

not as a welcome to us, but rather to resent intrusion, and to assert their seldom disputed right to live undisturbed in this remote and fairy realm. It was near this spot John Ploughman wrote the choice epitaph for his own tombstone, as given in an earlier chapter.

But my friends and I have come for business. Every point of interest is photographed. Then we enter the church. Two clergymen are conducting morning prayers with only the vergeress for an audience, and from her we learn what we can of its history. I must leave the reader to find this out for himself. But we found beneath the floor of one of the choir seats in the chancel 'a marble slab, with the brass of an esquire in armour, in a devout position, with a lion at his feet, and a scroll proceeding from his mouth.' We were told by one that this figure commemorates the death of some young esquire who was killed on or near this spot by a wild boar, and also that the last wild boar in England - the same, I think, that killed the squire was hunted down and slain here.

I was interested in many things in the little church, and not the least in the appropriate texts painted on the half dozen candelabras suspended from the roof. These were, 'The night is far spent, the day is at hand,' 'I am the Light of the world,' 'God is light, and in Him is no darkness at all,' 'The Lord is my light and my salvation,', 'The Lamb is the light thereof,' 'Make Thy face to shine upon Thy servant.'

But I must come to the incident connected with Okewood Church which has interested me most, and which will, I think, be attractive to the reader also.

In the course of the sermon suggested by this spot, the preacher alludes to the fact of this scene having suggested the subject of men gathering to the Saviour 'from every quarter.' He says, 'Seeking rest and health last week, I seated myself for a little while near a very

Hic jacet Edwardus de la Hale, armig. de Com. Surr. qui obiit hij°
die mensis Septembr
Anno D'ni Mills'mo. cccc xxxj° Cujus anime Deus misereatur
Amen.

rustic church which stands embowered in a wood, and as I sat there I moralised upon the various paths which led up to the church porch. Each pathway through the grass came from a different quarter, but they all led to one point. As I stood there this reflection crossed me: even thus men come to Christ from all quarters of the compass, but, if indeed saved, they all come to Him. There is a path yonder which rises from a little valley. The little church stands on the hill side, there is a brook at the bottom, and weir shippers who come from the public road must cross the rustic bridge and then ascend the hill. Such comers rise at every step they take. Full many burdened ones come to Christ from the deep places of self-abasement; they know their sinfulness, and feel it; their self-consciousness has almost driven them to despair; they are down very low, and every step they take to Christ is a step upwards. They have a little hope as they look to Him, and then a little more, till it comes to a humble trust; then from a feeble, trembling trust it rises to a simple faith, and so they advance, till when they stand near to Jesus they even reach to the full assurance of faith. Thus from sad distress and self-despair they come to the Lord Jesus, and He receives them graciously.

'Through the churchyard there was another path, and it ran uphill from where I stood, and therefore everyone who came that way descended to the church door. These may represent those who think much of themselves ... Every step these good people take towards Christ is downward: they think less of themselves, and still less ... The two paths I have mentioned were supplemented by a third, which led through a thick and tangled wood; a narrow way wound between the oak trees and the dense underwood and I noticed that it led over a boggy place, through which stepping-stones had been carefully placed for the traveller, that he might not sink in the mire. Many a seeker has found his way to Jesus by a similar path. Once more, I remarked another path which came in from the farmer's fields, through lands where the plough and the sickle are busy, each in its season; so that those who come from that quarter to worship come across the place of toil, and may fitly represent those who are full of earnestness and effort, but have as much need of Jesus as any. But if they ever come to Christ they will have to leave those fields and the plough and sickle of their own strength and submit to receive Jesus as their all.'

I trust this notice of it may cause many to read the sermon, and put it into the hands of such as are saying, 'Oh that I knew where I might find Him!'

I was frequently asked by him when we were together if I could suggest a text or a subject. I often did so. He not infrequently gave subjects to me; but I found that he usually forgot that he had done so, for he would often preach and print them soon afterward, which, as we were next door neighbours, put me in rather embarrassing circumstances.

He was issuing his shilling series of sermons, which contains *The Mourner's Comforter and Seven Wonders of Grace*; each volume having seven sermons. I suggested that as there are seven texts in which the heart of Christ is spoken of, he might preach another series, and make a volume on *The Heart of Jesus.* 'Ah!' he said, 'but how could I preach from, "Reproach hath broken My heart"? Yet I may do one day.' I am confident that if anyone was ever capable of preaching from it he was, for his sympathies with the suffering Redeemer were often so real and intense that he would weep even to sobs. At quiet communion services I have seen him with the deeps of his great nature broken up, and having, as he once said, 'to drink water to supply his eyes with tears.'' Mrs. Spurgeon, when well enough, would read to him concerning his Sunday subject on a

OKEWOOD CHURCH PORCH

ONE OF THE PATHS TO OKEWOOD CHURCH

Saturday evening; and when the subject related to the sufferings of the Saviour, as it often did, I know that both of them have been very greatly affected, and have wept tears of sympathetic sorrow together; so tender, and deep, and real was the love of both towards 'our own dear Shepherd' as smitten for the sheep. Our tutor, Mr. Rogers, told us when I was a student, that he thought it the one mistake in Mr. Spurgeon's ministry to describe so vividly the physical agonies of Christ. 'It never moves me,' said the old gentleman, 'to hear him preach as he sometimes does, so as to make the people see Christ beaten and bleeding before their eyes. If all souls were as responsive to Christ and as full of love to Him as his own, it would be different: but I fear whether such preaching does real good.' Yet have I seen, especially during Conference week, a very chastened and hallowed spirit produced in many by his setting forth Christ 'as crucified amongst us.' His Conference sermons on 'I thirst,' and on the miracles wrought by the Crucifixion, will never be forgotten by many.

He discouraged us as students from announcing *a series of sermons* on a given subject, and thought we ought to keep ourselves free for any subjects the Holy Spirit might suggest to us week by week. But he preached several series himself (yet without announcing them) on Thursday evenings with very great acceptance and effect. I heard each one in the volume of *The Mourner's Comforter*, and can testify to the enduring blessing they brought to my heart as to many others. He preached several on the Parable of the Sower as a consecutive series; but he did not finish the parable. One of these, on 'It lacked moisture,' was unusually fine. He had a series on the olive tree, and he thought of bringing out a book on the subject, but the design was never completed. I heard him on the text, 'Can the fig tree bear olive berries?' and I thought it the poorest

THE FAMOUS PREACHER 231

RUSTIC BRIDGE NEAR OKEWOOD CHURCH

PATH TO OKEWOOD CHURCH

I ever heard him preach, and for that reason it did me good, for I thought if he is not up to the mark sometimes, I will not be discouraged because I am not. I have known his great sermons to really discourage preachers. One brother minister, now in heaven, heard him on the text, 'He spake of trees, from the cedar tree that is in Lebanon even unto the hyssop that springeth out of the wall,' I Kings iv. 33, and he declared on leaving the church that he could never preach again. Another minister who was with him said to him, 'Don't say that; poor fellow, he could not help preaching grandly if he tried not to.' Well, if ever preacher was master of his work, Mr. Spurgeon was.

I heard him one Thursday evening on the text, 'Before Him shall be gathered all nations; and He shall separate them one from another, as a shepherd divideth his sheep from the goats.' The sermon is printed in Vol. xxi. Let the reader turn to it, and read the marvellous description of the gathering of the nations to the Judgment Seat. I give a few sentences to excite his interest. 'The dead of Egypt shall rise from their beds of spices, or from the earth with which their dust had mingled. The tens of thousands shall be there over whom Xerxes wept when he remembered how soon they would pass away. The Greek and the Persian they shall rise, and the Romans too, and all the hordes of Huns and Goths that swarmed like bees from the Northern hives. They all passed into the unknown land; but they are not lost, they shall each answer to the muster roll in the great day of the Lord.' One might almost fancy each sentence had been written out, and the whole sermon learned by heart, so beautifully are its sentences balanced, and so strong is the sermon as a whole. Yet I was told that he had been driven up with other work, and had but a few minutes in which to prepare this sermon. 1 have the original outline. It is written on a small envelope.

Journeying once from Scotland to London he asked if I had a text ready for Sunday myself. 'Yes, sir,' I said, '"And being let go they went to their own company,"' Acts iv. 23 - He at once gave me three main divisions.

I. God's people are a company.

II. The company feeling is strong when grace is strong.

III. The true believer carries this into effect.

'Now give me one,' he said. I suggested, 'For who is this that engaged his heart to approach unto Me? saith the Lord,' Jeremiah xxx. 2 I. 'Yes, yes, that's the one,' he quickly replied. 'Now tell me what you would say on it.' We talked the subject over, and at last he said, 'I am right for Sunday morning.' He preached it. It is printed in Vol. xxviii. No. 1,673. Another sermon he made in a railway carriage when we were coming up from Eastbourne. I mentioned the fact that he had no sermon on the shining of the face of Moses. The subject at once took with him; we chatted over it, and he preached from it the next day. One Saturday, as he often did, he bade me suggest a topic. I said, 'I have a specially good one, which I have kept for you, sir.' 'Give it me.' 'Bring me a minstrel. And it came to pass, when the minstrel played that the hand of the Lord came upon him,' 2 Kings iii. 15 'Whatever would you say upon that?' he said. 'Why, God's people get unfitted for service, and they need the cheerful music of promises, doctrines, and assurances to set them right.' 'Oh yes, I see; no, I cannot take such a subject as that from you.' 'It is yours,' I said; 'I give it you absolutely.' Then his soul seemed to glow, and he called out, 'O wifey, wifey, come here; listen to this subject. Now, Mr. Williams, tell Mrs. Spurgeon.' Mrs. Spurgeon was as delighted as her husband. In the middle of the next week I met a gentleman who had been to the Tabernacle on the Sunday morning previous. He said, 'Oh, I heard Spurgeon on

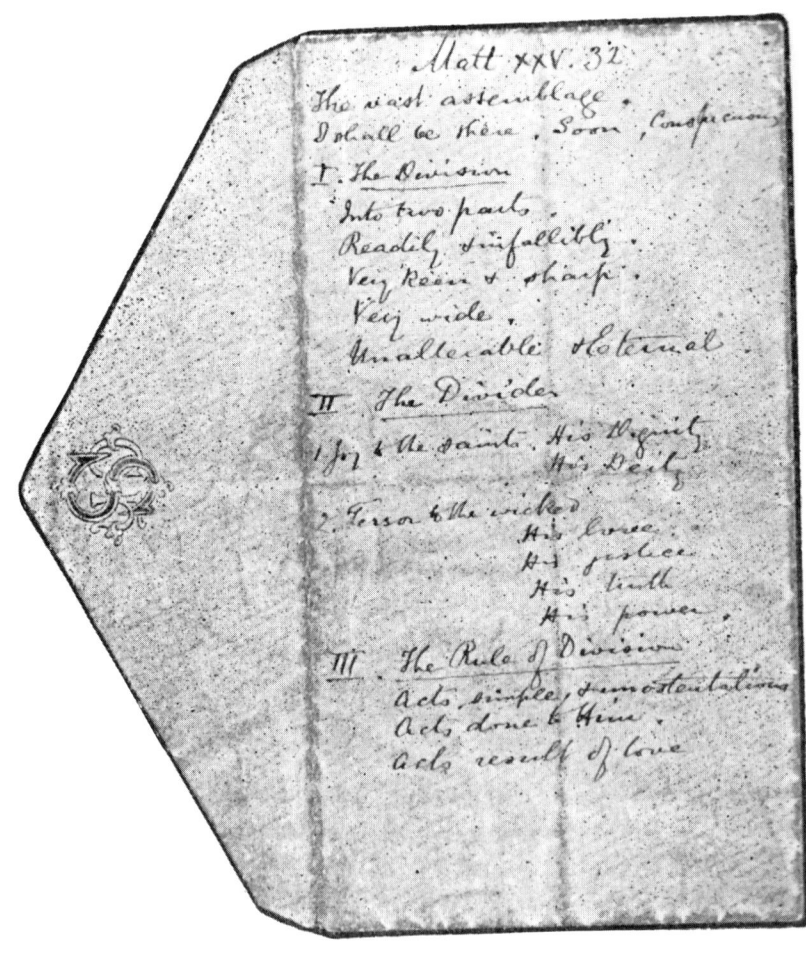

Sunday, and my heart has been dancing ever since.' 'What was his subject?' I said. 'Oh, the minstrel!' The next Saturday I went to see him, and as soon as I got into the study he said: 'Ah, friend Williams, Mrs. Spurgeon wants you, go to her.' I went, and she exclaimed, 'Oh, Mr. Williams, I do thank you so much for that subject. I have read the sermon, and it has helped me more than I can tell.'

A volume was issued by Mr. Spurgeon's publishers some time ago, entitled *Twelve Remarkable Sermons by C. H. Spurgeon*, and the 'The Minstrel' was the first in the book. I thanked God for this bit of indirect service I had been able to render through His honoured servant - so great, yet so humble that he gladly received such help as even I could give.

Another Saturday I suggested that the leper came to Jesus - others were brought or carried, but that he, though a loathsome leper, came; and how Christ honoured his marvellous faith. His face seemed to light up as with a supernatural glow, and he said, 'May I preach from that tomorrow?' 'Certainly, sir; I mentioned it for that purpose.' He did so. The next Saturday I went to see him. As soon as I got into his study, he exclaimed, 'Oh! Williams, I have a glorious bit of news for you. Through that subject you gave me a harlot of the deepest dye was converted. She got in amongst the crowd, and hid herself as much as possible; but the Lord brought her there, and saved her. She has now gone home to her broken-hearted mother. I have such a letter from her. Isn't that glorious? This is the sort of thing I like to live for.'

I think I was most surprised at his sermonising power in connection with a sermon he preached on Easter Sunday morning, 1890. I was at his house on the Saturday, and he asked if I had a subject for him. 'Yes, sir,' I said, 'but I am afraid it is a tough one, rather.' 'What is it?' 'Well, tomorrow is Easter Sunday, and this subject will be just the thing if it bites.' It is in Acts iii. 15 - 'The Prince of Life.' I made a few suggestions, not many; the subject did bite, and he preached the next morning a sermon of unusual power and ability, as the reader may ascertain for himself, if he will obtain it. It is No. 2,159.

It would be easy for me to go on thus to a great length; but I leave it with the reflection that I ever feel grateful as I look through the volumes of this master of pulpit utterance for having been allowed to suggest sermons which he in his own inimitable way gave as a precious permanent heritage to the Church of God and to the world at large.

We were talking over the subject of 'Friendship with God' one Saturday, and the next morning he preached on it. He asked me who above all living persons I considered to enjoy Abraham's dignified privilege of being God's Friend. I suggested the name of a good old saint known to both of us. 'No,' he said, 'he is *a* friend of God, but not *the* friend. I say Mr. George Muller, of Bristol. How near he lives to God! and he gets anything from Him he cares to ask for.'

Mr. Rogers once said to us in college, 'A minister's interest in his sermon is before he preaches it, the people's interest in it is after he has preached it.' But Mr. Spurgeon seemed at times more interested in his sermon after preaching it than before. He would often go over his discourse point by point, with evident delight at having been so graciously helped. He found great joy in this, the main business of his life. The last sermon he thus rehearsed to me was delivered on Lord's Day morning, September 14, 1890. He came from the service to the house of his devoted friend and deacon, Mr. William Higgs, to dinner. I was asked to spend an hour or two with him. It was to me a singularly happy season. He had preached that morning with his whole nature consciously bathing in the sunshine of Divine love;

and the charming manner in which he went over the subject, which had afforded him such joy as he preached it, has made it to live with me until this hour as few other sermons have done.

Great as were the known results of his sermons, I believe the unknown were far greater. I have discovered many of his converts who had never told him of the blessing his word had been to them. In 1864 he preached one Thursday evening from 'Ye are complete in Him.' A gentleman who has for some years been one of my deacons was converted through that word, but Mr. Spurgeon knew nothing of it until I told him. A worthy and devoted elder of my Church heard him preach nearly thirty years ago on, 'Speak, Lord, for Thy servant heareth,' and became a changed character from that hour, but the preacher had never heard of it. I count among my own choice friends a gentleman in the country who has exceptional abilities, and occupies a public position, who was led into peace and spiritual liberty through reading the sermon entitled, 'Only trust Him! only trust Him!' It is in Vol. xxvii. No. 1,635. My friend ought to have told Mr. Spurgeon, but he did not. He, however, joined a Christian Church in his own neighbourhood, and became a prominent member of a Mutual Improvement Society, often reading papers and taking part in debates. He became an ardent politician, and often spoke at political meetings; but he had not spoken definitely and directly for his Master when he heard Mr. Spurgeon preach on Lord's Day evening, February 13, 1887. Let the reader judge, therefore, his feelings when the preacher said: 'There is a young fellow who ought to be preaching the gospel: he made a very pretty speech, the other night, at a Mutual Improvement Society; he can speak well enough as a politician, and if there was an election, we should find him talking fast enough; but he is dumb so far as the Church of Christ is concerned. Come out, brother!' He did come out, and has often spoken for his Master since.

A good-sized volume might easily be filled with interesting incidents connected with the delivery of the sermons.

Preaching one Sunday evening against self-righteousness Mr. Spurgeon personified a man in the audience saying, 'I don't think much of your religion, nor of your religious men, after all. Why, there is a man sitting behind you whom you think a lot of, and you have made an officer of him: and I can remember the time when he had scarcely got a shirt to his back.' To this the preacher replied, 'My dear fellow, don't you be too fast, you have surely no cause to boast; perhaps your mother remembers the time when you had not any shirt to your back.'

A young fellow, a friend of mine, was sitting right in front of the pulpit one Sunday, and dropped off to sleep. The atmosphere of the building, when it was densely crowded, was often very heavy. Mr. Spurgeon saw him sleeping, and tried to wake him by speaking straight at him, and by dropping his voice to a whisper and then raising it to a thunder-clap. But the sleeper slept on serenely. At last Mr. Spurgeon remembered the youth was fond of coursing, for he knew him well, and he introduced an illustration in which greyhounds were seen running after a hare. The young gentleman soon opened his eyes at this; and once having got him awake, Mr. Spurgeon said he took care not to let him sleep again.

Years ago a deacon, now in heaven, used occasionally to *nod* as he sat on the platform. Mr. Spurgeon, turning round once, saw him. He said to another deacon as he was leaving the pulpit, 'You have a cold, Brother --, your breathing was so heavy I thought you would wake up Brother --.' The nodding deacon is said never to have nodded thus again. This gentle rebuke effectually cured him. But a sleepy hearer was a very rare sight at the Tabernacle. I was told that there was a very valid excuse for the deacon who dropped off. But so heavy did the atmosphere at times become that if the preaching had been less interesting than it was, one could scarcely have wondered if others had slept. I was present on the Sunday evening when Mr. Spurgeon preached the sermon entitled 'The ear bored with an awl.' The subject was our choice of perpetual service, and our reasons for it. The sermon was partly autobiographical. He said: 'This is a memorable night to me. Pardon my speaking of myself, I cannot help it. It is exactly twenty-four years ago this night that I put on the Lord Jesus Christ publicly by baptism, avowing myself to be His servant.' And he proceeded to speak of his own personal determination to serve on to the end. In speaking of the reasons for this, he mentioned our love to our Master, then our love to our Master's household. His brother, Dr. James Spurgeon, was sitting in the pulpit behind him. The preacher turned right round, and putting his hand on his brother's shoulder said, with his eyes filled with tears and his voice charged with tenderness, 'My brother, how could I leave your God, to be separated from you, whom I have loved so long, so well?' It was singularly affecting. Dr. Guthrie has recorded his disappointment on hearing Mr. Spurgeon that he had not more pathos. But he was full of it. There were not many dry eyes in the congregation that night. No written account of the service could adequately represent what was seen and felt. The brother well deserved that public avowal of affection on the part of the one he helped so much and served so faithfully. Mr. Charles Spurgeon could never have written so much, nor served other Churches so nobly and frequently, had his brother not given himself to attend to the details, and even drudgery, of Church work. The great preacher knew this, and expressed to me his gratitude to God for such a helper. When Mr. Spurgeon was arranging with his brother to become co-pastor, he said to him, 'You know, brother, if two men are on a horse *one must ride behind.*' 'Yes, brother,' said Mr. James, ' I will ride behind and hold you on.'

His humour often came to the fore in his preaching. He was preaching one night on Hannah. 'Ah!' he said, 'this is the sort of woman God trusts to bring up His Samuels. Look at that young fop; when he was young he was his mother's *duck*, and now he has grown up to be her goose.'

Speaking on 'A garment of praise,' he said, 'Everybody must wear the garment of praise which fits him best; mine is so big I could put any half-dozen of you in the pockets.'

Reproving laziness, he said, 'Oh, you say, "The Lord will provide"; yes, He will very likely provide you a place in the parish workhouse, or else in the county jail.'

'If crowds come to hear a preacher, some are ready to say, "Oh, they are running after a man." What would you have them run after - woman?'

His prayers in the pulpit were as helpful as any part of the service. The opening prayer on a Sunday morning was often as remarkable for its beauty of language as for the tender devotion of spirit it breathed. Here is a portion of one of many which linger after twenty years and more in my memory and heart.

'Our Gracious God, we Thy children bless Thee for this Thy day; placed not now at the end of a week of toil, but at the very beginning of it, for we have not to labour to obtain the day of rest, but Thou dost give us to rest first, and then bid us go and work in the strength received. Thy day has often been to us as the couch of time, whereon our weary spirits have found repose, and as the flower beds in the garden, the rest of the week being but as the walks between. May we this day walk among the spice beds where the Rose of Sharon sheds His fragrance. May all our natures be perfumed with His love.'

Closing his *long* prayer one Sunday morning he said, 'And now, O God, ere we close our prayer we would enter by faith within the veil, we would stand upon the glassy sea before Thy great white throne all pure and lustrous. Wings have we none wherewith to cover our face and feet, as the angels do, but we take the robe of spotless righteousness our Saviour wrought and cast it around our soul, and thus adorned, we bow, and worship, and adore. Glory be unto Thee, O God the Father, the Covenant God of Thy people; Glory be unto Thee, O God the Son, who redeemed us from death by Thine own dear blood; Glory be unto Thee, O God the Holy Ghost, the Author of our light, our life, our joy. Unto the one Eternal Jehovah, infinite in power and glory, do we render now undivided homage, and by Thy grace will do so while we have any being.'

His prayers at the Monday evening prayer meeting were often full of remarkable power. It seems to us a pity they were never taken down. The reading of them would have afforded glimpses into his inner life which his sermons scarcely give, and would also have helped many in their approaches to the mercy seat. A small volume has been published, however, and is greatly valued by not a few devout spirits.

At one of the Monday evening prayer meetings, some twenty-two or three years ago, he was urging the people to try and do more to influence the neighbourhood for good. He said, 'I cannot go visiting, but I will try to do my share in another way.' He then read some lines he had written, which were to be printed on large posters and put up wherever a suitable space could be found. I suppose those lines are forgotten by most who read them, while most of Mr. Spurgeon's admirers never heard of their existence. I think I can reproduce them; I quote from memory.

ETERNITY

Where wilt thou spend eternity? -
Nay! don't tear down the hill;
The question means but good to thee,
And will be answered still;
To shun the light, or shut the sight,
Thy cup of wrath may fill.
Where wilt thou spend eternity?
Don't say, 'I cannot tell';
The life thou leadest now will end
In heaven - or else in hell.
Oh! friend, bethink thee well.

C. H. SPURGEON

All these things serve to show how capacious his mind and heart were, and how passionately he longed to serve his generation according to the will of God. In his preaching and speaking he was witty, so as to interest souls; but he was wise to win them too. Tears were seen on the cheeks of penitents far more often than smiles on delighted listeners. Every faculty he possessed was laid under tribute to the one great aim of winning men to God. That I so often had my soul brightened by his sanctified mirthfulness, so often quickened by his glowing earnestness, so often counselled by his wisdom and love, were privileges for which I am increasingly grateful to God, and by means of which, I trust, I have been rendered more serviceable to men.

CHAPTER IX

SERMON SAPLINGS

I POSSESS a number of original outlines by Mr. Spurgeon, and I copy several of them, giving them exactly in the form in which they were written. The sermons preached from some of them are printed, others are not. I give the number of those printed, that the tree may be seen which grew from the sapling.

Job xxviii. 7

The ways of the miner are beyond the eye of eagle or track of lion. Such too is -
I - THE PATH OF DIVINE WISDOM
1. In reconciling predestination and free agency.
2. In accomplishing His designs in Providence.
3. In achieving His purposes of grace.
4. In future displays of His glory.
  He is so great.
  We are so little.
  Our power so wasted, so prejudiced.
  Our surroundings so dark.
  Our time so short.

Let us not despond at our ignorance.

Let us not arraign the Lord at our bar. Let us not spend our time in speculation.

II - THE PATH OF THE TRULY WISE

1. His entrance on that path.
2. His walk along it.

Neither reason, imagination, feeling, nor bravado, nor self-sufficiency.

3. His perseverance in it.
4. His trials in it.
5. His triumphs in it.
6. His communion along it.
7. His final steps in it.

Psalm xxvii. 9. Printed No. 1,144

In times of distress a choice of helpers may be a difficulty; while choosing the physician the patient dies. Here the Psalmist is shut up to the Lord alone. In turning to the Lord it is well to have a suitable, simple, available, and powerful plea which we may urge at all times. The plea before us could not be used with our fellow-creatures, but it may with the Lord. Dr. Duncan and the way beggars came round him.

I - EXPERIENCE GRATEFULLY TELLING HER TALE

1. Help in the struggle of finding peace.
2. Help in the solitude of neglect.
3. Help in early battles of faith. Mother and child.

4. Help in escape from his enemy.
5. Help in raising up friends.
6. Help out of trouble into which unbelief had placed him.
7. Help under strong temptation.
8. Help in dark hours. Ziklag. I Samuel xxx. 6.
9. Help opportune, sufficient, constant, gracious, many sided.

II - NECESSITY URGENTLY PLEADING EXPERIENCE
1. Therefore it is consistent with Thy holiness.
2. Therefore it is clear that Thou hast power.
3. My appeal is to Thy wisdom.

All the past will be lost. Jacob's seven years for Rachel. Israel in the wilderness.

4. I urge Thine immutability. The sun, the fountain.
5. I plead Thy love.

The conductor and traveller in centre of glacier.

The wife, the child.

III - EXPERIENCE SOUNDLY INSTRUCTING FAITH
1. Thou hast been my help so long.
2. Thou hast been my help so constantly. Birds in the cage.
3. Thou hast been my help so singularly in deep trial. Fear not trial, death.
4. Thou hast been my help so gloriously to Thyself. This is a plea which the self-justiciary cannot urge.

This the trembling sinner may urge in a measure.

Common mercies.

Spiritual mercies.

Solomon's Song ii. 16. Printed No. 1,190

Last Sabbath we began at the beginning, and spoke of the turning point; now we rise toward the crown of Christian life, and take the believer in one of his best moods. At such a time Jesus rises high in the soul, for He is the thermometer of the soul's heat. What He has done, is doing, and will do, are the only important matters to us. Love is blind to all but her Beloved.

We see the heart -

I. - DELIGHTING TO HAVE JESUS

1. *His existence matter of fact.* Love realises Him, and the sweet influence thereof banishes doubt.
2. *Our love to Him the subject of consciousness.* We feel the flame. It is the greatest actuating force in our whole life.
3. *Our possession of Him proven.* The promise, the gift of the Father, the marriage, our faith, &c. Jacob. Thomas.

We are sure that He is ours when we feel love to Him.

4. *That possession the main treasure of our lives.* Not earthly things, nor even spiritual, but Himself.

Is He not unrivalled? Is not our possession unrivalled?

5. *The contemplation of the fact our main delight.*

Whatever else we may or may not have, He is ours.
He is altogether ours, in all His nature, work, &c.
He is absolutely ours, so that we may use and enjoy.
He is always ours, never forsaking or denying.
He is ours, to each in the singular, personally.
As our love would have Him, such is He.
This, then, is the basis of the Christian life.

SERMON SAPLINGS

II. - DELIGHTING TO BELONG TO JESUS

1. *This may be proven.* Creation, election, redemption, calling, consent, marriage, choice.
2. *It bestows great honour.* To think we should be worth anybody's having, and especially His!
3. *It is true absolutely.* Not any goods, time, powers, &c. alone, but I and all that I am.
4. *It is true evermore.* Today, tomorrow, in life, in death.
5. *It is true as a matter of fact.* I surrender my whole being to Him! Do you?
6. *It involves wondrous privilege.* Provision, protection, preservation, perfecting, heaven.

'They also whom Thou hast given Me be with Me,' &c.

It is a wonder altogether that *I* am His!

Yet a sure matter of fact.

We belong not to the world, nor to the Church, nor to a party, much less to self or Satan. We are entirely, exclusively, and irrevocably our Lord's.

III - DELIGHTING IN THE VERY THOUGHT OF JESUS

1. Where is He? Among the pure in heart both in heaven and in earth. High favours. Grace and glory . Frail yet provided for.
2. What is He doing?   Feeding Himself in joy.
                        Feeding the glorified.
                        Feeding His saints.
3. What shall I do?   Get among the lilies.
                        Be myself a lily.

This, then, is one joy that Jesus is in His Church, and is happy in her. This is our source of strength, our hope of victory, our consolation in distress.

O Lord, come among us now.

Sinner, remember who she was who thus sung.

Black, cast out by her mother's children, made a vineyard keeper. In the winter, rain, and in the holes of the stairs. Yet singing thus:

> O be mine still; still make me Thine;
> Or rather make nor mine nor Thine.[1]

Gal. v. 6. Printed No. 1,280

The great doctrine of Paul was salvation through faith. This also was the great truth of the Reformation. It is now being testified on all hands and with remarkable clearness. It is so divine that it is no wonder that it seems strange - strange even to the anxious. I speak to them with a view of clearing difficulties.

I. - WHAT IS THIS FAITH?

1. As an act it is not different from BELIEF, only it believes God's testimony, and as a consequence -
2. It includes *reliance* upon Him who is set forth as a Saviour.
3. It is not a mere reliance upon Divine mercy, neither is it a belief that you are saved, but an *acceptance* of Jesus as saving men from sin.

---

[1] 'Let mine melt into Thine.' See Sermon.

II. - ANSWER OBJECTIONS AGAINST ITS BEING THE WAY OF SALVATION

1. God has in very truth appointed it.
2. Those who truly believe are evidently saved from their sins.
3. If it be a licentious method, why do not the licentious adopt it?
4. The other method cultivates selfishness, and leaves the heart untouched.
5. In other matters the principle has acted well. Pinel and the lunatics. The King, Isaac Hopper, and Cain.
6. Think how it would operate on yourself.
7. Remember who works it and what it works.

III. - THEN ITS OPERATIVE POWER

1. It changes man's view of God, and so begets love instead of fear or hate.
2. This produces repentance for having treated Him so ill.
3. It reveals the price paid for pardon, evokes gratitude, and so love.
4. Love to the Saviour leads to desire to please Him.
5. Leads also to imitation of Him.
6. Leads to love to all mankind, and so to the relative virtues.

To the newly saved. Prove your faith by your love. Answer these objections by your lives.

2 Samuel vii. 18-22. Printed No. 1,166

David was overwhelmed with the mercy which the Lord heaped

upon him. He went into the place of access and sat resting, waiting, and adoring in the immediate presence of the Lord his God. There he mused, and saw further into the covenant (see Acts ii. 30), and saw that Jesus was promised to be of his race.

In like manner let all the saved have boldness of access, and sit down and feel as he did. We note:

I. - HIS HUMILITY

In the presence of the mercy of God he remembered -
1. The lowliness of his origin. 'I took thee from the sheepcote.'
2. The littleness of himself 'Who am I ?' He saw in himself no natural qualification or excellence.
3. The lack of all desert. Even after he had been a ruler. Much less before.
4. His utter nothingness before the Lord God. Nothing humbles us like a sense of Divine love.

II. - HIS WONDERING GRATITUDE

1. At what had been done. Preservation while in sin, calling out of sin, renewal of heart, pardon, justification, sanctification, adoption, &c., &c.
2. At what was promised. Laid up as well as laid out. Preservation, provision, preparation, aid in death, eternal glory, 'a great while to come.' He speaks as if each mercy eclipsed all preceding.
3. At the manner of it all. Not after the law of man, or the custom of man, but after the law of THE MAN. Grace so free, so forgiving, so constant, so bounteous, so divine is amazing.

III. - HIS LOVE

1. Love struck dumb by an unspeakable gift. What shall we say of these things?
2. Love in childlike accents mentioning its own name. 'What can David say more?'
3. Love communing, wishing to speak 'unto Thee,' and glad to appeal to Him who knows its heart.
4. Love obediently styling itself a servant.
5. Love adoring the 'Lord God.'

IV. - PRAISE

1. For the freeness of grace, 'according to Thine own heart.'
2. For its fidelity, 'for Thy word's sake.'
3. Its connection with Jesus, 'the Word.'
4. Its greatness, 'all these great things.'
5. Its condescending familiarity, 'to make Thy servant know them.'

V. - HIGH THOUGHTS OF GOD

1. He extols the Lord as great.
2. He adores Him as greater than all others.
3 He worships Him as greatest of all.

This is a sweet result of meditative gratitude.

God too great for us to grieve by sin. ------ for us to doubt.

So great that we count nothing too great for Him.

------- desire all to worship Him.

------- expect to see Him proclaimed King over all the earth.

John viii. 29. Printed No. 1,165

Our Lord was the lone advocate of right and truth; those who followed Him were rather His care than His help. His enemies were many and powerful, yet He went calmly on, for God was with Him. We need the same blessing, and therefore let us gaze upon Him, and learn from Him how to secure it.

I. - LET US ADMIRE OUR MEDIATOR

1. His Incarnation. 'Lo, I come,' &c.
2. His obscure life. 'This is My beloved Son.' Father's business. He grew in favour with God and man.
3. Pleased with Him at His baptism, when He began His public ministry; in the wilderness angels came.
4. With His life of veiled glory, at Tabor, it thundered. Isaiah xlii. 21. He kept the ceremonial, moral, and mediatorial law.
5. His death. It pleased the Lord to bruise Him. Voluntarily submissive, believing, triumphant.

Now is the Father pleased to place in Him all fulness, and He is pleased that He should give it out to sinners and to all His saints. All the works of Jesus please the Father. His intercession and forerunning. His reign and judgment.

The Father is with the work of Jesus now.

What encouragement to workers! What hope to sinners!

II.- LET US IMITATE OUR MODEL

1. This will imply that we are ourselves pleasing to Him. This can only be in Jesus, and we are there only by faith. If we

act by self, we are in the flesh, and cannot please God.

2. There must be an absence of that which does not please. Pride, sloth, unwatchfulness, anger, murmuring, being cumbered, unbelief, &c., must be eschewed.

3. There must be an intent, a study, an anxiety to please. Much lies in the spirit of our acts. In obedience to the Holy Spirit we must consult, yield to, and delight in, the will of the Father.

4. There must be a copy of the Lord Jesus, whose life was pre-eminently a life of prayer; and fellowship with God. Love, gentleness, and goodness to men.

Doing good zealously.

Self-denial, and seeking God's glory.

Going without the camp.

Complete absorption in the Divine will.

5. We may further learn from Scripture.

From the example of Enoch, walking with God.

Psalm lxix. 31, Heb. xiii. 16. Sacrifice of praise.

I John iii. 22. Love to the brethren.

Col. i. 10. Every good work, increasing in knowledge of God, long-suffering, and patience, &c.

6. These things must be actually done, and not merely talked of and admired. Practical holiness is that which pleases. To know, and not to do is sin.

7. This must be always. At home, in society, in secret, in business, &c.

8. This will secure to us communion with God and His powerful aid.

It will make us influential over others.

Calm in our own souls.

Happy in the life of heaven.

Is this too high a model? Then you love not Jesus.
Is this impossible to reach? Do you doubt the Holy Spirit's power?
Have you failed? Grieve over it.
Will you labour for it? He waits to help you.
He worketh in us mightily.

Luke ii. 29

Flesh and blood had not revealed this unto him. Men naturally cling to life. They are neither for heaven nor willing to leave earth. This is a work of grace for which we may say, 'Thanks be unto the Father.'

I. - THAT EVERY BELIEVER MAY BE ASSURED OF DEPARTING IN PEACE

1. He has seen God's salvation.
2. He is at peace.
3. He is God's servant.
4. Hitherto all things have been 'according to Thy word.'

It shall be alike departure out of confinement - cage - servant waiting - out of toil.

It shall be appointed in the same manner.

It shall have the same benediction.

II. - THAT SOME BELIEVERS FEEL A SPECIAL READINESS

1. *When their graces are vigorous.*
Faith brings clusters from Eshcol.

Hope sees the whole before her eyes. Pisgah.
Love ascends to it like smoke from the flame.
Humility possesses it. 'The poor in spirit.'
2. *When assurance is strong.*
Without this men cannot be willing to go. Faith, understanding, self-examination, witness within.
3. *When communion is near and sweet.*
Haste, my Beloved. Longing for the marriage. Showing Himself through the lattices.
4. When their hold of the world is loose.
5. When their work of blessing God, avowing faith, testifying of Christ, and blessing others is done.
6. When they see the prosperity of Zion.

III - THAT THEY ARE WORDS TO ENCOURAGE US TO THE LIKE READINESS

Psalm xxiii. 4. A walk through a shade, attended, fearless, comforted.

Psalm xxxvii. 37. 'Mark the perfect man, and behold the upright: for the end of that man is peace.'

Psalm cxvi. 15. 'Precious in the sight of the Lord is the death of His saints.'

Isaiah lvii. 2. 'He shall enter into peace: they shall rest in their beds, each one walking in his uprightness.'

I Cor. iii. 22. 'All are yours.'

I Cor. xv. 55. 'Where is thy sting?'

Rev. xiv. 13. 'I heard a voice from heaven saying unto me, Write, Blessed are the dead which die in the Lord.'

Now to sinners. Negative. - I Cor. vi. 9, Rev. xxi. 8.

Luke xxii. 32

Satan has a deadly hate of all good men. That he is sure to sift them if permitted. This is permitted for their good and God's glory.

I. - OBSERVE THE GRAND POINT OF ATTACK

1. It is the vital grace essential to the soul.
2. It is the chief grace leading the way.
3. It is the nourishing grace.
4. It is the preserving grace.
5. It is the effective grace.
6. It is the most obnoxious to Satan, because the most glorifying to God.

II. - OBSERVE THE PECULIAR DANGER

1. There was a faith in his Master, so that he repented at a glance.
2. He did not go and hang himself.
3. He did not forsake his brethren.
4. He was soon at the sepulchre.

Doubt the truth of it all. Doubt your own interest. Doubt possibility of pardon. Doubt His love.

III - OBSERVE OUR GRAND DEFENCE

1. Intercession prevalent, prevenient, pertinent.
2. Intercession of one who opposes Himself to Satan, His prayers to Satan's desires.

3. Intercession of which the issue is so anticipated that He gives directions to be followed.

Zech. xii. 10-14

I. - THE GRACIOUS MOURNING

1. Evangelical.
2. Continual.
3. Personal.

II. - THE SECRET CAUSE

1. Effectual.
2. Extensive.
3. Secret.

III. - THE VISIBLE MEANS

The fact of His sorrow.
    that we caused it.
    that it atoned for us.
Now we see the evil of sin.

From such outlines as these Mr. Spurgeon preached the marvellous collection of sermons contained in the forty volumes of the *New Park Street* and *Metropolitan Tabernacle Pulpit*, as well as the many others published in his one shilling and three and sixpenny series. *Over sixty million four hundred thousand of the weekly issue have been printed and sold.* Messrs. Passmore & Alabaster keep about two millions of these weekly sermons always in stock; and the printing of fresh supplies is ever proceeding. Only a few days ago one order alone was received for *one hundred thousand copies.* In addition to this a fresh sermon is issued each week, the demand for which is as great and keen as ever. The one issued for the week in which I write, June 9, 1895, on 'Adorning the Gospel,' I had the joy of hearing delivered, and can testify to the freshness and power with which it came home to the hearts of the congregation; and in reading it one feels this power anew. It is remarkable for its simplicity of language, and equally so for its freshness and beauty of thought. It is No. 2,416. The publishers had sufficient of these sermons in manuscript when Mr. Spurgeon died to continue the publication of the weekly number *for ten years at least.* So that if life be spared we may yet become the possessors of *fifty* volumes or more of C. H. Spurgeon's sermons, printed week by week through half a century. There has been nothing in all sermon literature to come anywhere near equalling this, either as to the number issued or yet as to their circulation.

The productions of no other preacher's heart and brain ever kept a great printing and publishing firm constantly engaged with the issue of his works alone. I have been through the publishers' store rooms; these contain many tons of Mr. Spurgeon's works, which are in constant demand. *John Ploughman's Pictures* has reached its 140th thousand; and *John Ploughman* is now in its 400th thousand. For a shilling book, dealing with moral and religious matters, this sale is, I believe, absolutely unprecedented. The choice volumes *Morning by Morning* and *Evening by Evening* have enjoyed a sale of over two hundred and ten thousand. These have been amongst the most useful *sermon saplings* many a preacher has possessed; thousands of sermons have been delivered which were suggested by these charmingly gracious chapters; while of the yearly volumes the Chairman of the London Congregational Union for 1895 said: *'No preacher's library was complete without them.'*

Among the many other volumes of Mr. Spurgeon's which contain *seed thoughts for sermon saplings* is one now out of print, and very rarely to be met with; though I was fortunate enough years ago to pick up a copy. Its title is, *Smooth Stones taken from Ancient Brooks*, by the Rev. C. H. Spurgeon. As a frontispiece the volume has a likeness of Mr. Spurgeon - taken, I should say, when in his *teens*. It is adorned also with a picture of the house where he was born. In the preface there is a brief account of *Thomas Brooks*, and an analysis of this great Puritan preacher's farewell address to his congregation. The volume consists of choice extracts from Mr. Brooks' works, and it shows how eagerly and thoroughly the young preacher at Park Street had read the six large volumes which comprise this author's valuable writings. In the sermons of Mr. Spurgeon which he preached years ago there are many beautiful thoughts and aphoristic expressions which were evidently the result of the study of Brooks.

The four volumes of Mr. Spurgeon's Sermon Notes, containing in all two hundred and sixty-four outlines of sermons, from which he preached, are by far the most helpful books to preachers in sermon-making which he has published. With each skeleton are given extracts from some of the best authors; and illustrations also, which bear directly on the subject in hand, so that if the preacher feels he would rather treat his subject in his own way - and all surely ought to feel this - he has nevertheless many practical suggestions he may very justly appropriate both for exposition and adornment.

THE END

A SHORT INDEX

Articulation, some confound loudness ... 188.
AV Bible, book for the people, 38.
Baxter Richard, art of pleading,186,190.
Bear, forbear,213.
Bowls, he used to play,89.
Bunyan John, his style like Christ,97.
Calvin John, suffered from forty nine diseases,168.
Chicken broth,134.
Christmas and New Year Cards,62.
Church, smallest in England,106.
Clean, be in your person,182.
Court, woman in court,168.
Cowper Wm, spirit broken in boyhood,173.
Dancing, I don't like dancing,164.
DD, title of,139,157.
Death, Ruskin's view of,70.
Dress, best way to dress,79.
Emancipation Oak,108.
Funny stories, telling them,103.
Gough John B, Temperance reformer,40.
Hall Bishop's Contemplations, buy that book!146.
Havergal F R, charming poems of,80.
Hood Paxon, his friend,204,234.
Horses, called his horses Jews,90.
Hymn, always have one of praise,194.
Ireland, his review on,54.
Jonah, how he was sucked in,134.
Marriage, services a civil agreement,197.
Mind The, eight sets of thoughts at same time,97.
Moody and Sankey, two blessed men,56,225.
Muller George, lives near to God,56,265.
Neuralgic, suffered from,226.

Newton John, on Calvinism,145.
Paul, like Wesley & Calvin,59.
Pilgrim's Progress, keep at your fingertips,190.
Plymouth Brethren, reject our idea of ministry,167.
Prayer, long prayers injure prayer meetings,138.
Preachers, blundering in grammar,82.
Preaching, effective preaching,138.
Punctual, preachers should be,167.
Puritans, got term 'bias of will' from bowls,89.
Queens Hotel Eastbourne, his favourite, 106.
Radstock Lord, baptism regeneration,58.
Reading in pulpit, perfection is to talk it,135.
Ruskin John, attends Tabernacle,69.
Scotland, on holiday,114.
Scott Sir Waiter, greatest mind created,53.
Scott Thomas, his Commentary not much help,136.
Second Coming, preach the first coming,166.
Sermon, No 227 signally owned of God,238.
Sermon, two texts in one sermon,187.
Sermons, preach about forty minutes,165.
Servant man. Old George,75.
Shaftesbury Lord, a friend,72.
Sunday Schools, visit frequently,194.
Taylor J, Cross but dimly seen in his works,166.
Wages, increasing them and mine,197.
Watts lsaac, on prayer,178.
Wednesday, his day of rest,90.
Wells James, Surrey Tabernacle,60.
Whitefield G, on Matthew Henry's Commentary,144.
Working hours, early or late? 88.